ARTIST TRANSCRIPTIONS PIANO

Oscar Peterson TRIOS

Transcribed by Forrest "Woody" Mankowski

Photo courtesy of Al Gilbert, F.R.P.S., Toronto, Canada

ISBN 0-634-07776-7

HAL•LEONARD® CORPORATION

7777 W. BLUEMOUND RD. P.O. BOX 13819 MILWAUKEE, WI 53213

Visit Hal Leonard Online at
www.halleonard.com

Oscar Peterson
Biography

Oscar Peterson was born August 15, 1925 in Montreal, Quebec, Canada. His parents were immigrants from the British West Indies and the Virgin Islands. His father, Daniel Peterson, was boatswain on a sailing vessel when he met Olivia John in Montreal, where she worked as a cook and housekeeper for an English family. They decided to remain in Canada, get married, and start a family.

Oscar was the fourth of five children. Originally taking an interest in the trumpet, a childhood bout of tuberculosis switched Oscar's emphasis to the piano under the tutelage of his father and later his sister, Daisy. His musical talent soon surpassed the capabilities of home teaching, and he was sent outside of the home to study. Oscar studied with the gifted Hungarian classical pianist Paul de Marky, and a warm and respectful musical friendship developed between the two.

In 1947, Oscar formed his first Canadian trio and retained this format of performance for the next several years. During this time, he remained dedicated to establishing a true trio sound. At an appearance in the Alberta Lounge in 1949, impresario Norman Granz heard him and enticed him into making a guest appearance at Carnegie Hall with his all-star concert troupe known as "Jazz at the Philharmonic." Leaving the audience awestruck, Oscar returned home for a year, then rejoined JATP as a steady member in 1950. He commenced recording with Norman Granz's Mercury label, and formed his first American duo with bassist Ray Brown.

In 1950, he was awarded the *DownBeat* Award for Best Jazz Pianist. He would go on to garner this award twelve more times during his career. He continued his extensive touring of the United States, and later, as a musical ambassador for the Canadian government, he toured Europe, Africa, South America, the Far East, and even Russia.

During these busy touring schedules, he formed a jazz school in Toronto, known as the Advanced School of Contemporary Music, which attracted students from all over the world. While on tour, he would conduct seminars and, amazingly, found time to compose his "Canadiana Suite," a salute to Canada, which was recorded with his trio and released worldwide.

Oscar has recorded with many of the jazz greats over the years. His varied albums with these giants include recordings with Louis Armstrong, Ella Fitzgerald, Count Basie, Duke Ellington, Dizzy Gillespie, Roy Eldridge, Coleman Hawkins, and Charlie Parker, but it has been the recordings with his various trios that have brought him recognition from numerous places around the world.

In recent years, Oscar has been devoting more and more time to composition. His "Hymn to Freedom" became one of the crusade hymns during the civil rights movement in the United States. He has composed music for motion pictures, including the Canadian film *Big North* for Ontario Place in Toronto, as well as the thriller *Silent Partner*, for which he won a Genie Award in 1978. His collaboration with

Norman McLaren, titled *Begone Dull Care*, won awards all over the world. Oscar also composed the soundtrack for the film *Fields of Endless Day*, which traced the Underground Railroad used by African-Americans escaping to Canada during the slavery era. In addition, he has worked with the National Film Board of Canada.

Oscar followed his motion picture work with a ballet commissioned by Les Ballets Jazz du Canada, which included a special waltz for the city of Toronto titled "City Lights." Other compositional projects included "A Suite Called Africa" and a salute to Johann Sebastian Bach's 300th birthday, written for trio and orchestra. These were followed by the "Easter Suite," which was commissioned by the BBC of London and performed with a trio on Good Friday, 1984, via nationwide television. This particular production is still broadcast annually. He also composed music for the opening ceremonies of the 1988 Calgary Winter Olympic Games. In addition to all of these, Oscar has composed over 300 other tunes, most of which have been published.

Oscar has appeared on a wide array of television productions, and has hosted his own specials where he interviewed and played with a variety of guests. His widespread appeal gave way to an unusual range in personalities that included Anthony Burgess, Andrew Lloyd Webber, Tim Rice, and Edward Heath, the former Prime Minister of England.

Oscar prefers not to use his celebrity to sway political opinions, yet he remains dedicated to the belief that his native Canada has a responsibility in leading the world in equality and justice. With this in mind, he has taken a firm stand to promote recognition and fair treatment for Canada's multi-cultural community. Because of his efforts in this field, Mr. Peterson was inducted as an Officer of the Order of Canada in 1972. He was promoted to Companion of the Order, Canada's highest civilian honor, in 1984.

In 1993, Oscar was awarded the Glenn Gould Prize. He was the third recipient of the Prize, the first with a unanimous decision, and the first ever from the realm of jazz. Over the years, Mr. Peterson has been awarded many honorary degrees, and a host of other awards, including the Praemium Imperiale (the Arts equivalent of the Nobel Prize), the UNESCO International Music Prize, the Queen's Medal, the Toronto Arts Award for Lifetime Achievement, the Governor General's Performing Arts Award, and most recently the President's Award from the International Association for Jazz Education.

Despite a mild stroke in 1993, which at first debilitated his left hand, Oscar recovered to continue his yearly pattern of worldwide concert tours, recordings, and composition.

Mr. Peterson resides in the quiet city of Mississauga, Ontario. As a citizen he insists on his privacy, which he jealously guards. His hobbies include fishing, photography and astronomy, and he is an avid audiophile and synthesist. His home contains his own private recording studio, where he can work but still be able to enjoy his family life. His passion for life, love, and music is stronger than ever.

◆

n

Oscar Peterson
Contents

Alice in Wonderland
from Walt Disney's ALICE IN WONDERLAND

Words by Bob Hilliard
Music by Sammy Fain

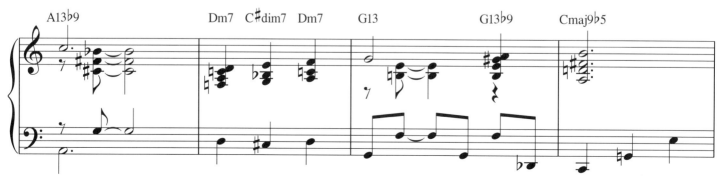

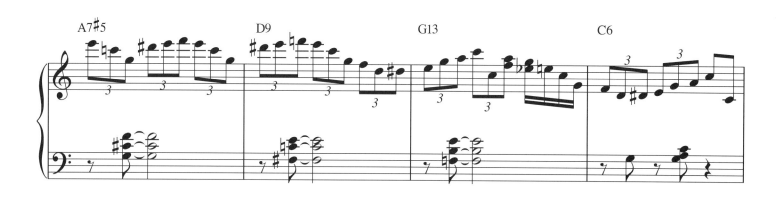

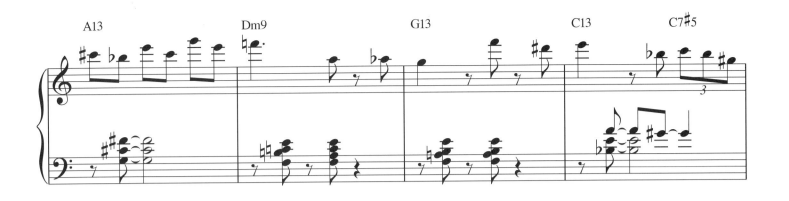

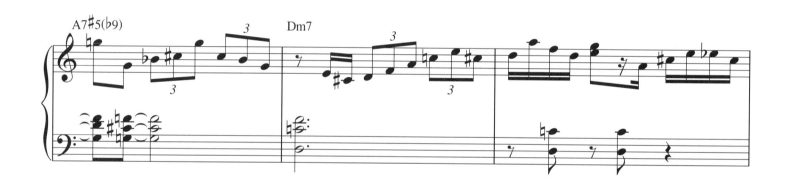

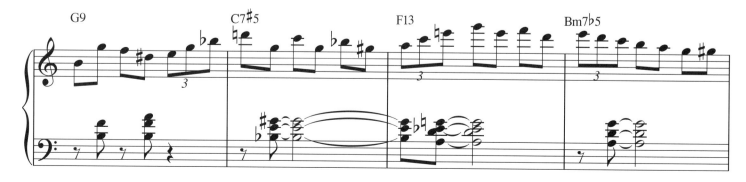

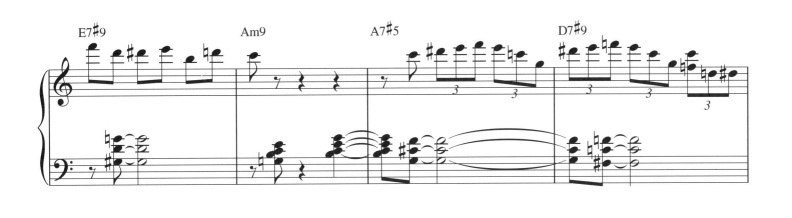

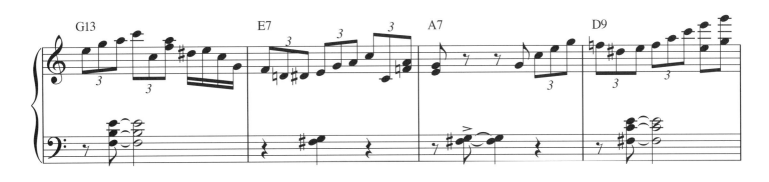

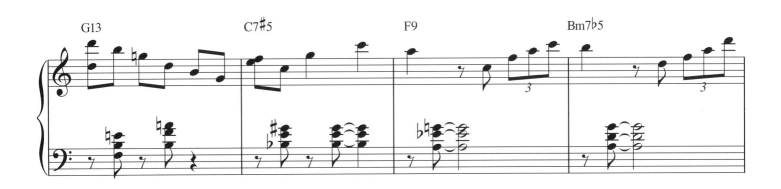

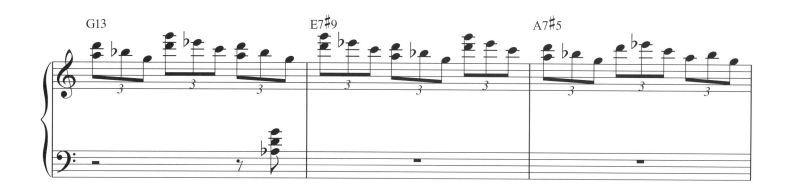

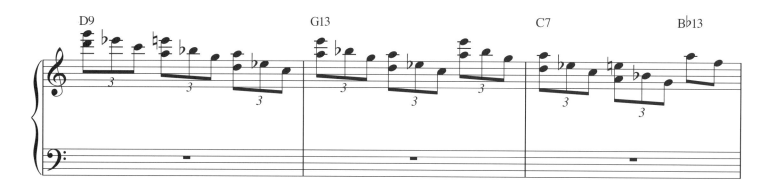

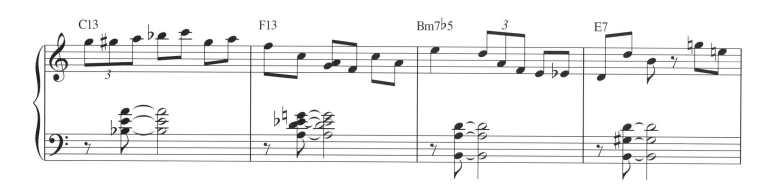

14

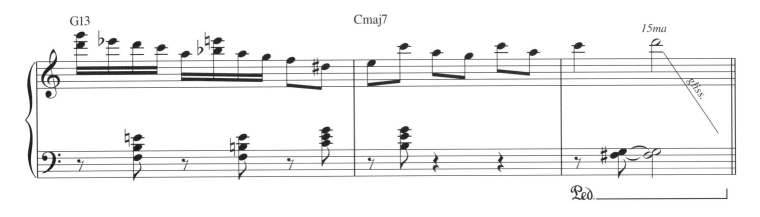

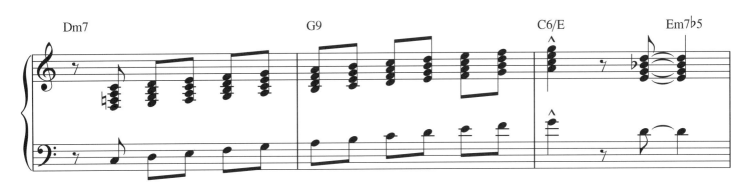

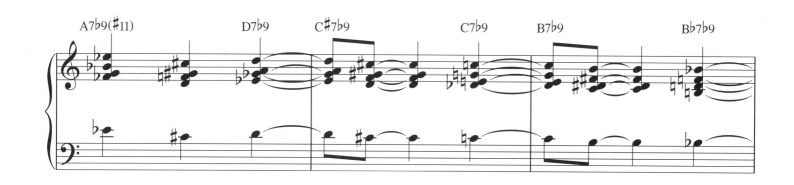

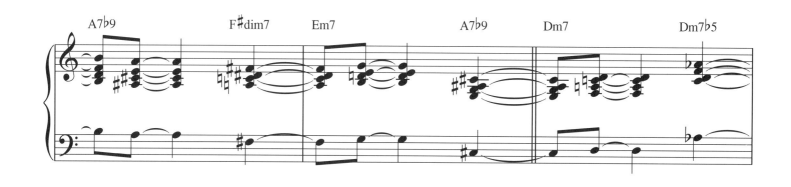

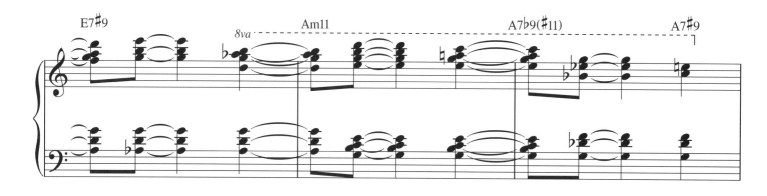

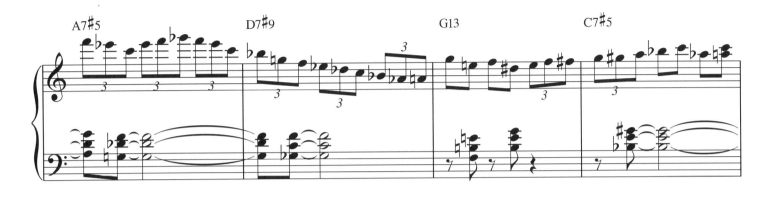

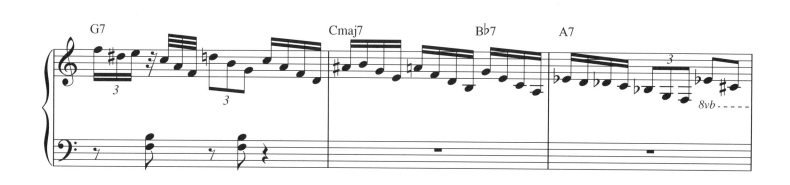

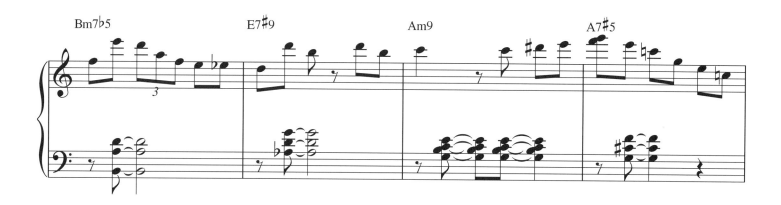

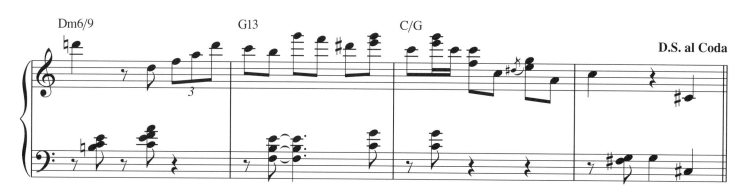

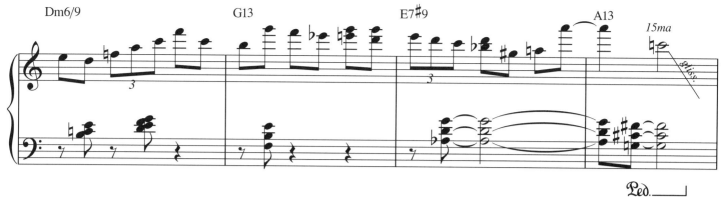

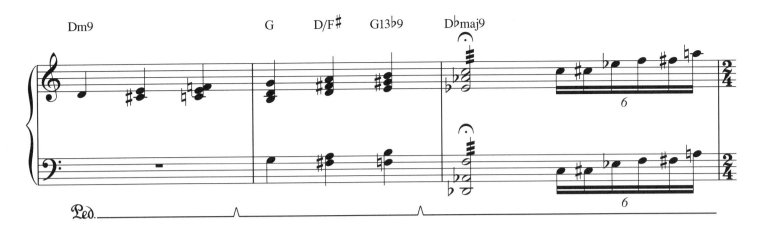

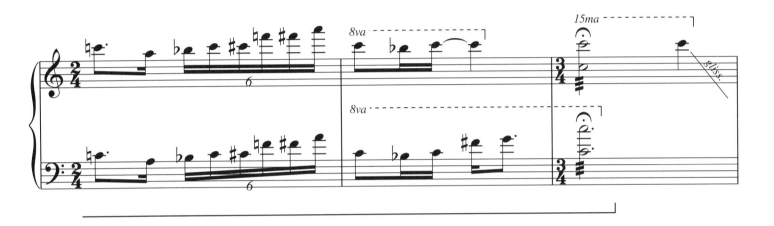

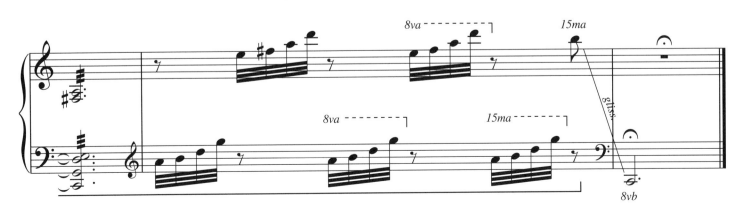

Blues Etude

By Oscar Peterson

Moderate Swing ♩ = 134

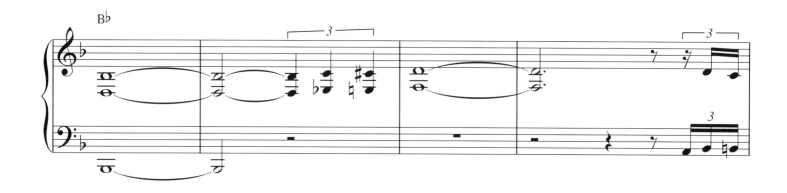

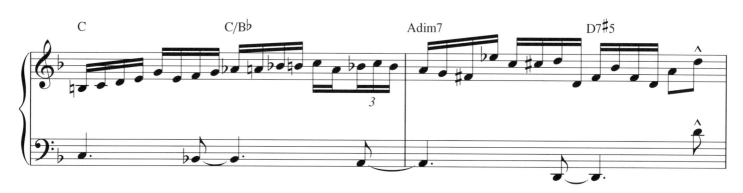

Bright Swing ♩ = 240

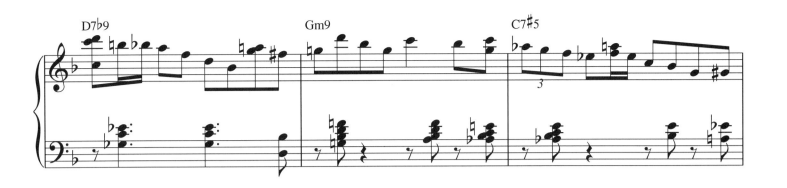

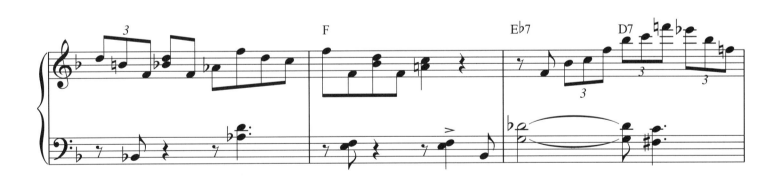

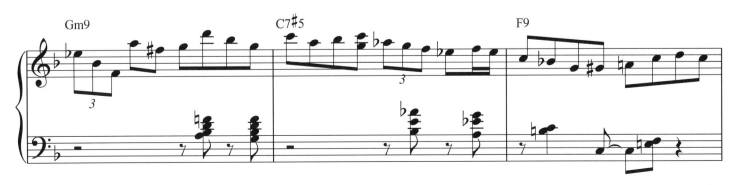

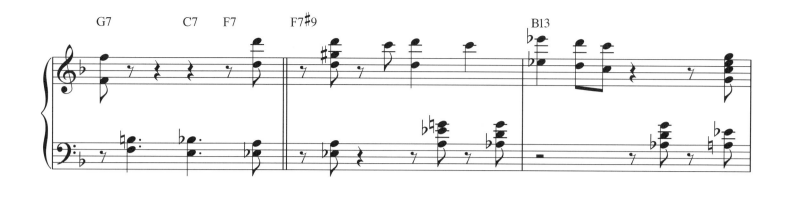

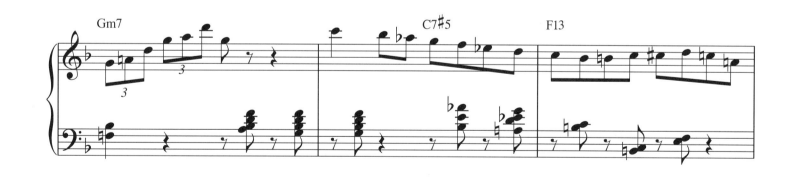

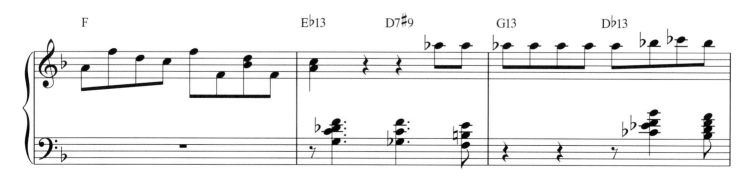

28

Bass Solo

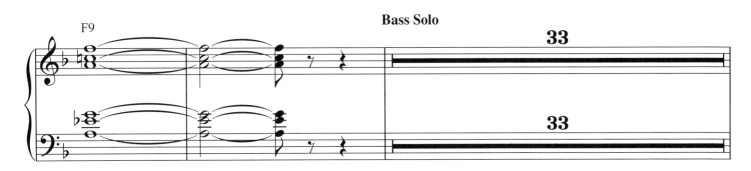

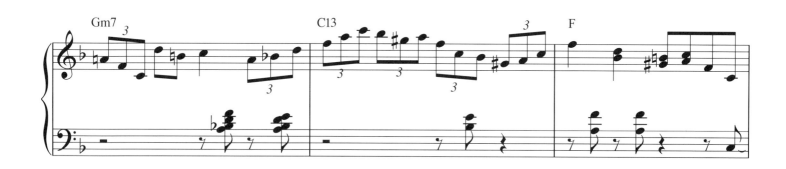

Drum Solo

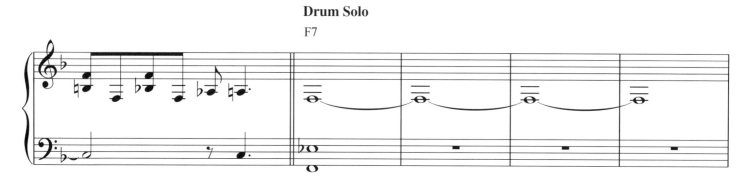

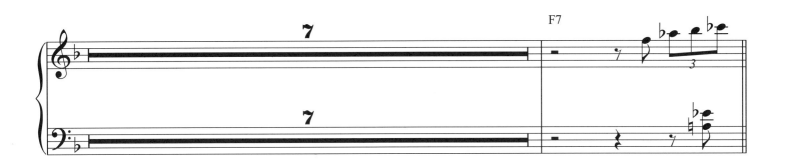

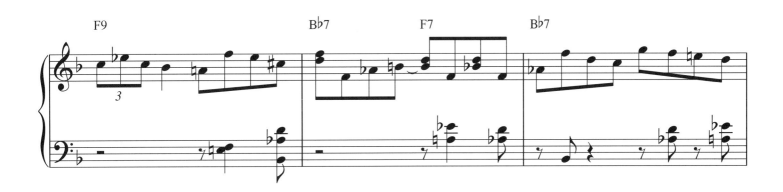

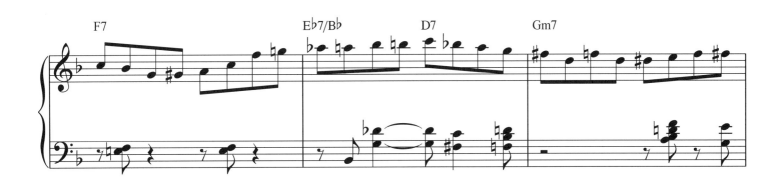

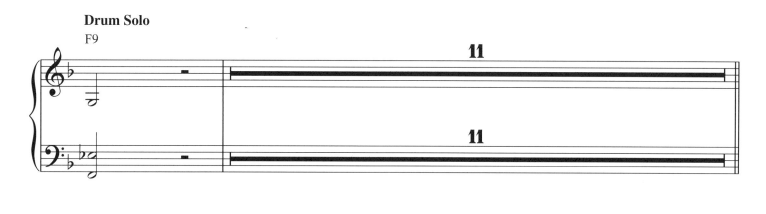

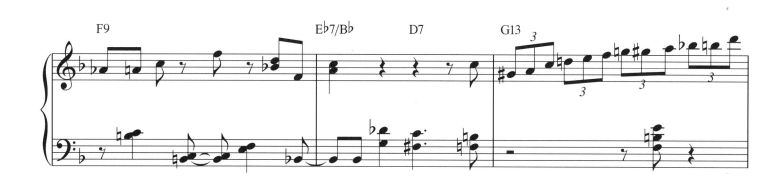

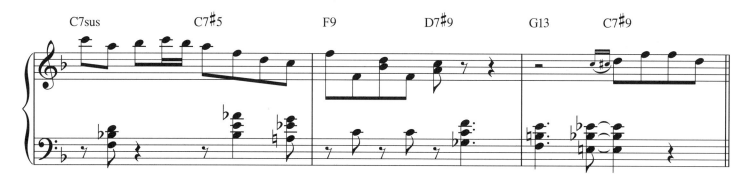

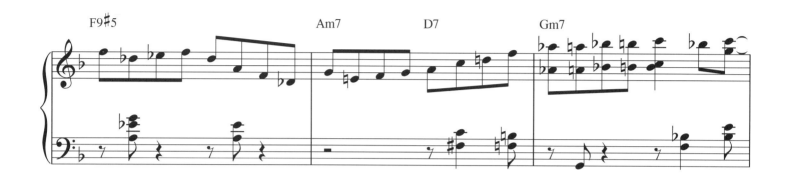

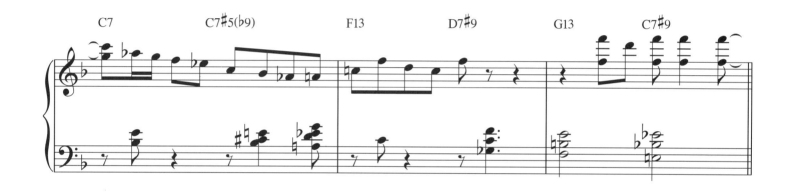

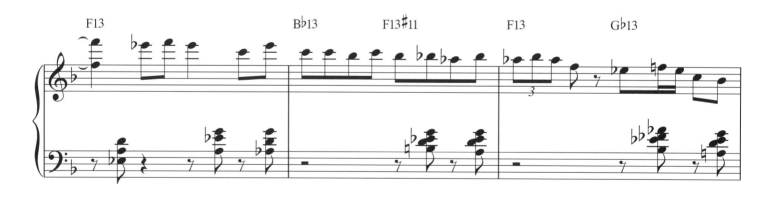

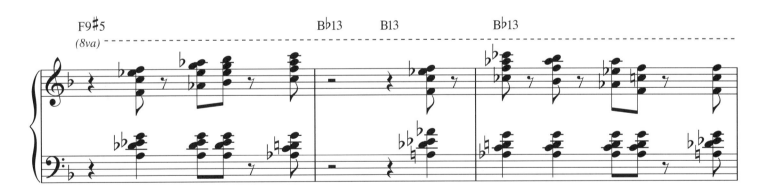

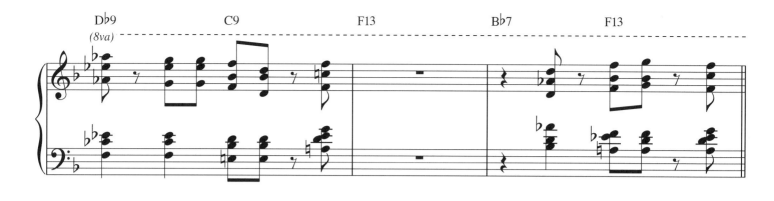

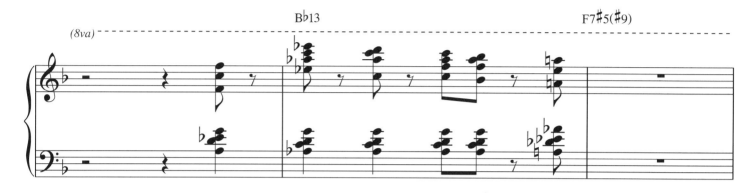

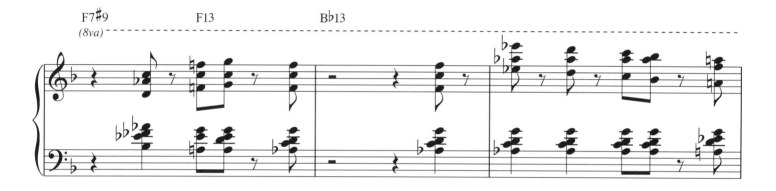

Moderate Swing ♩ = 148

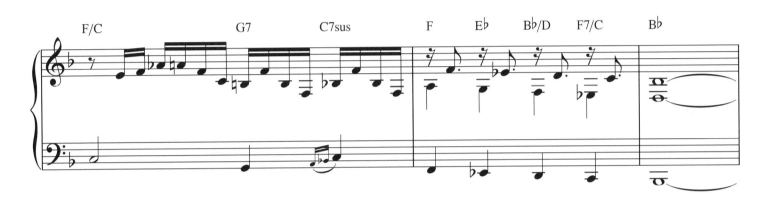

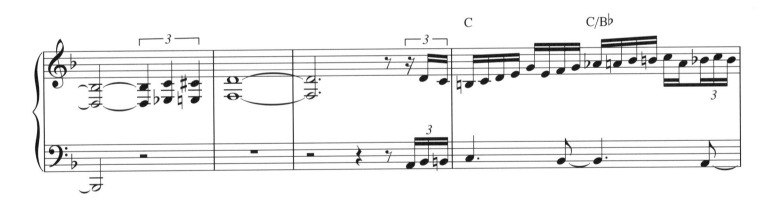

Cheek to Cheek
from the RKO Radio Motion Picture TOP HAT

Words and Music by Irving Berlin

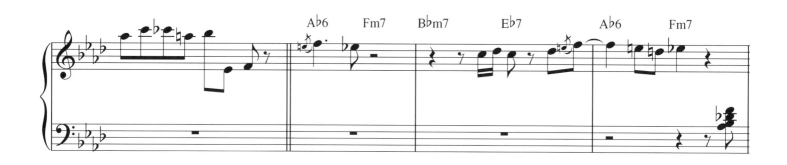

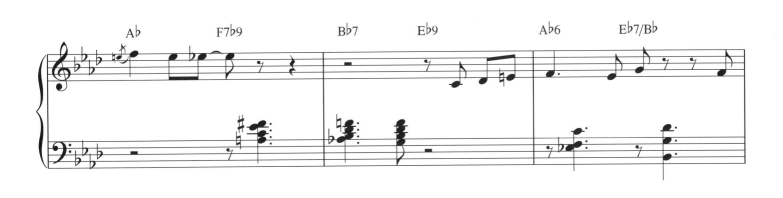

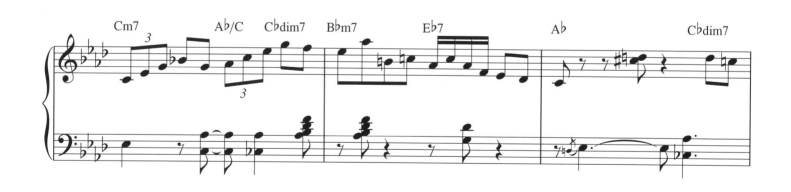

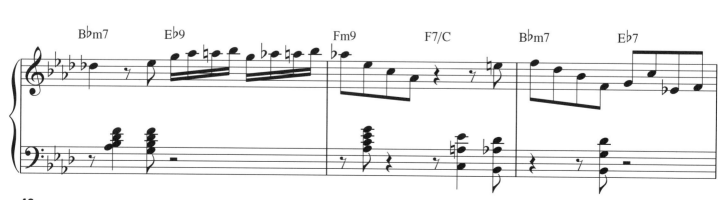

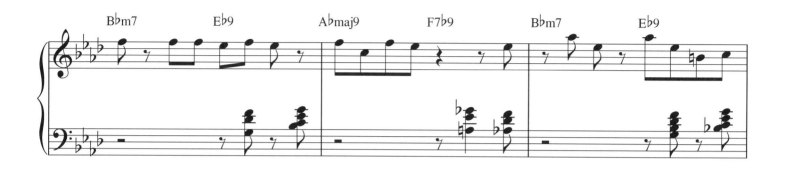

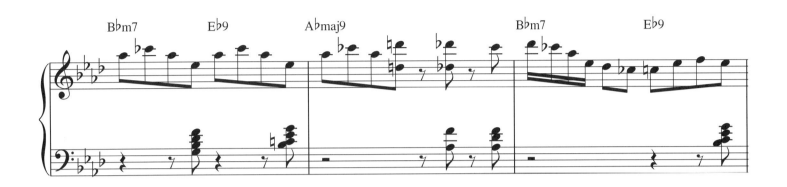

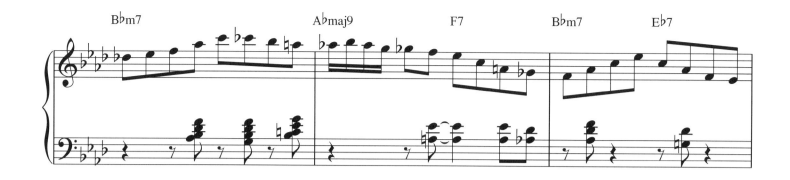

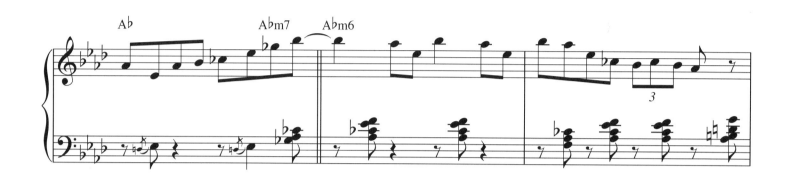

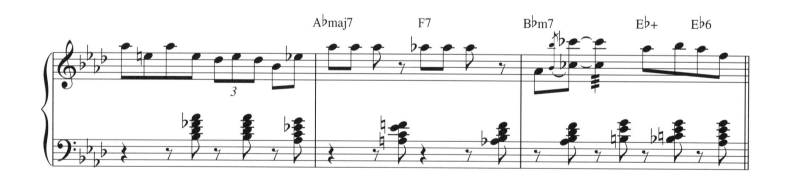

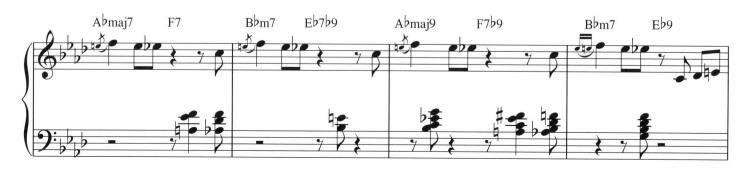

Emily

Music by Johnny Mandel
Words by Johnny Mercer

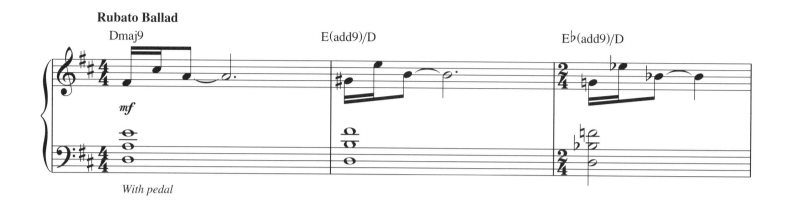

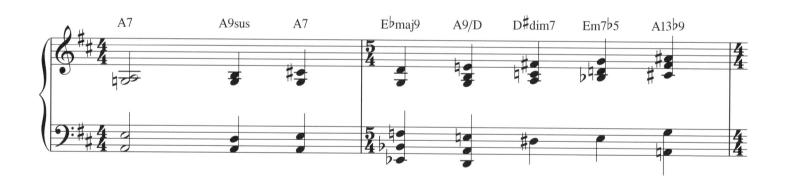

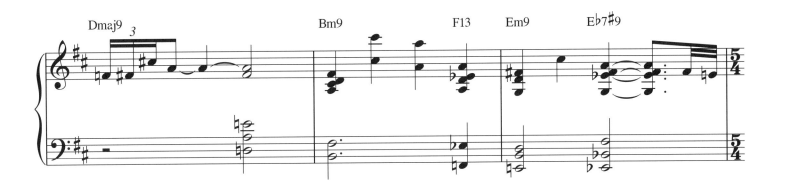

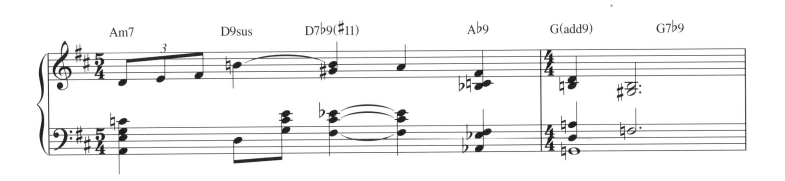

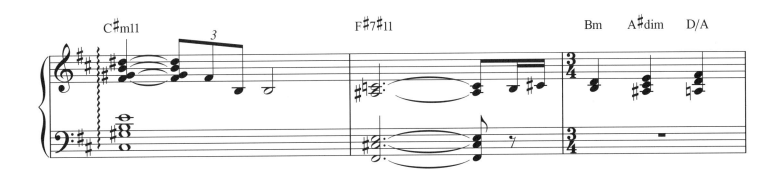

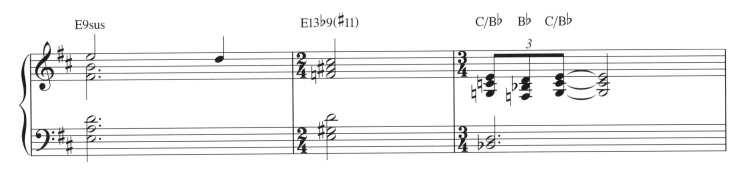

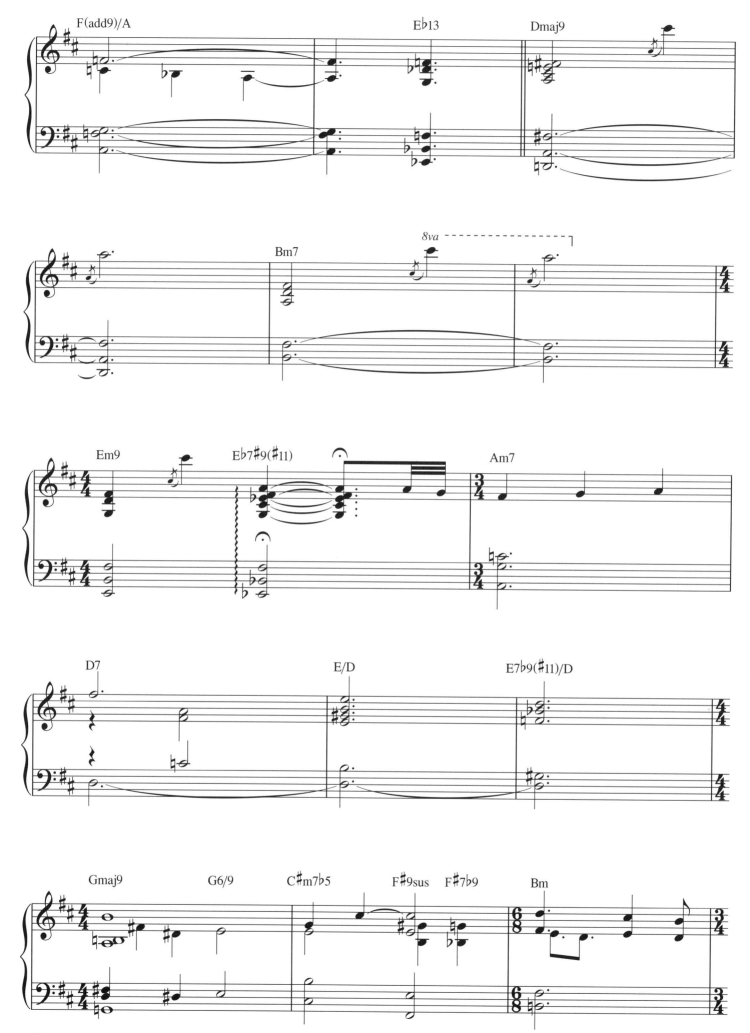

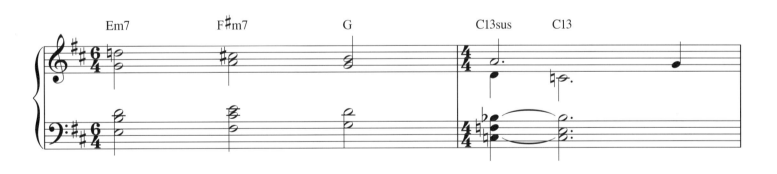

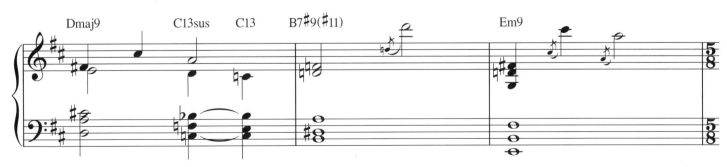

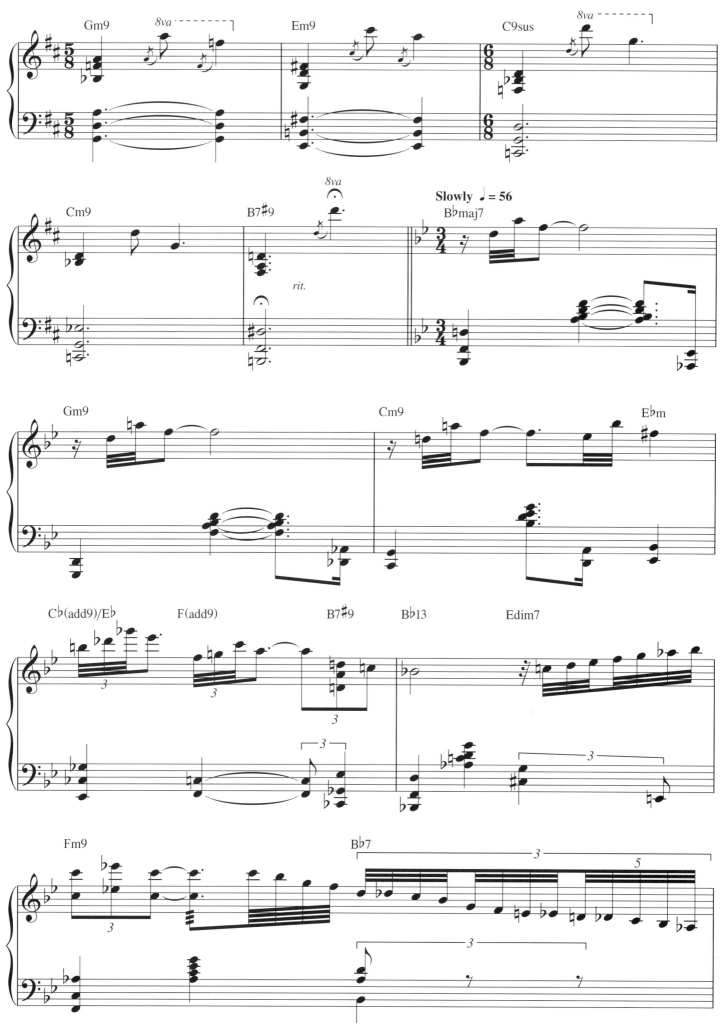

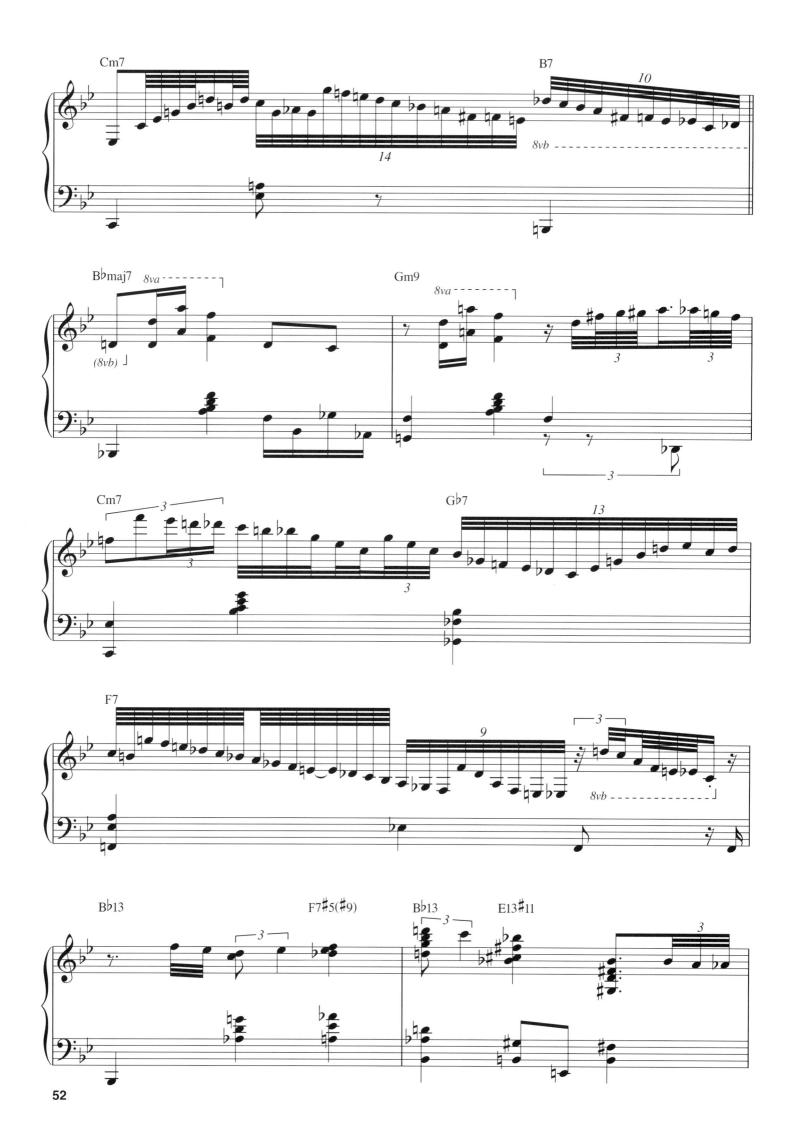

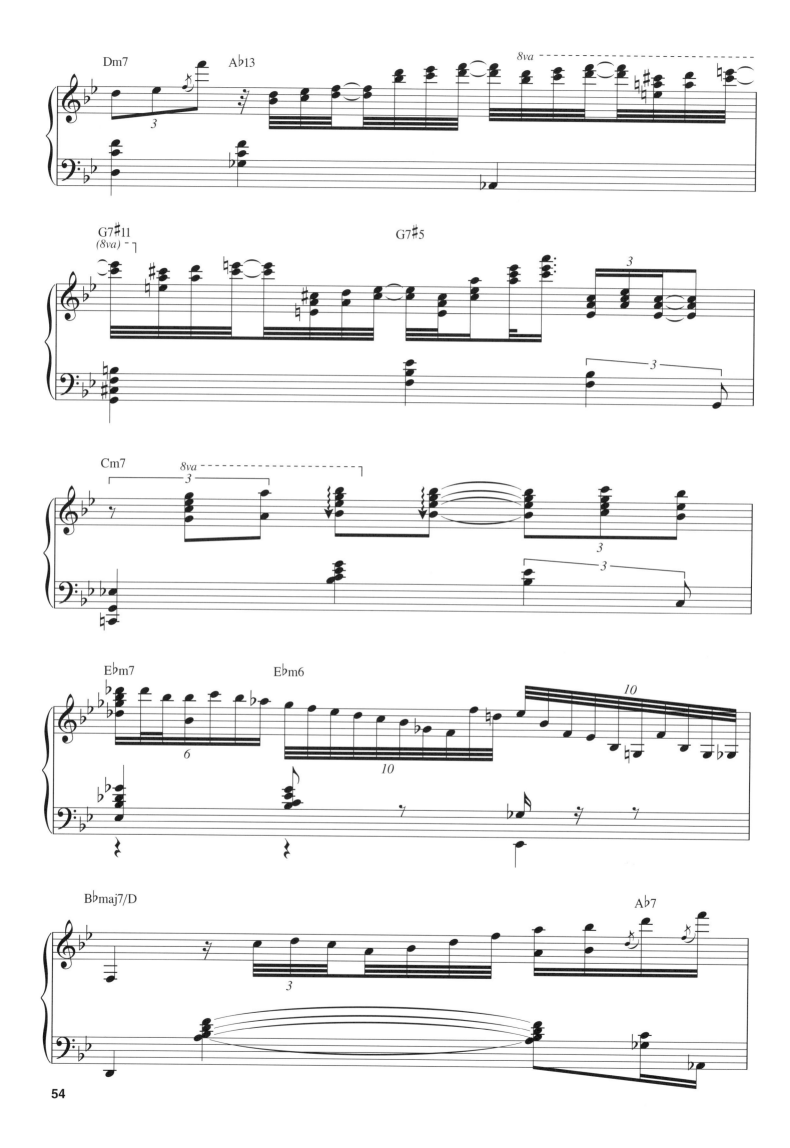

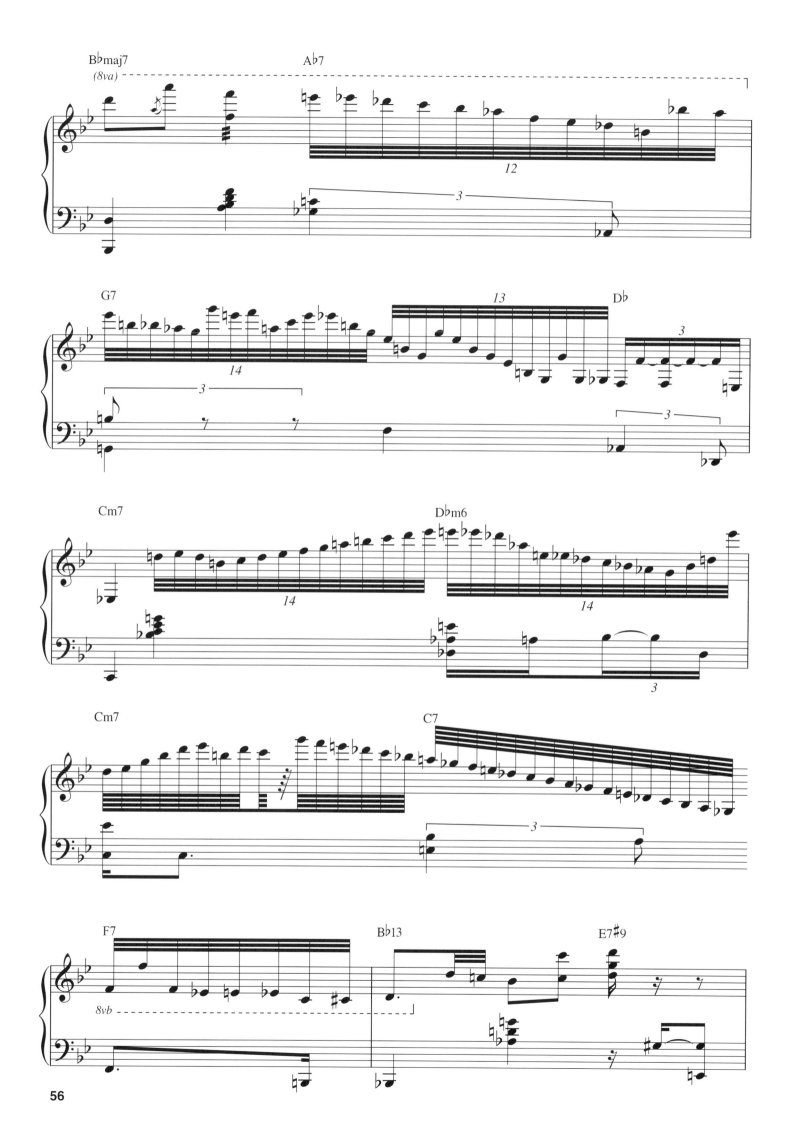

Hymn to Freedom

By Oscar Peterson

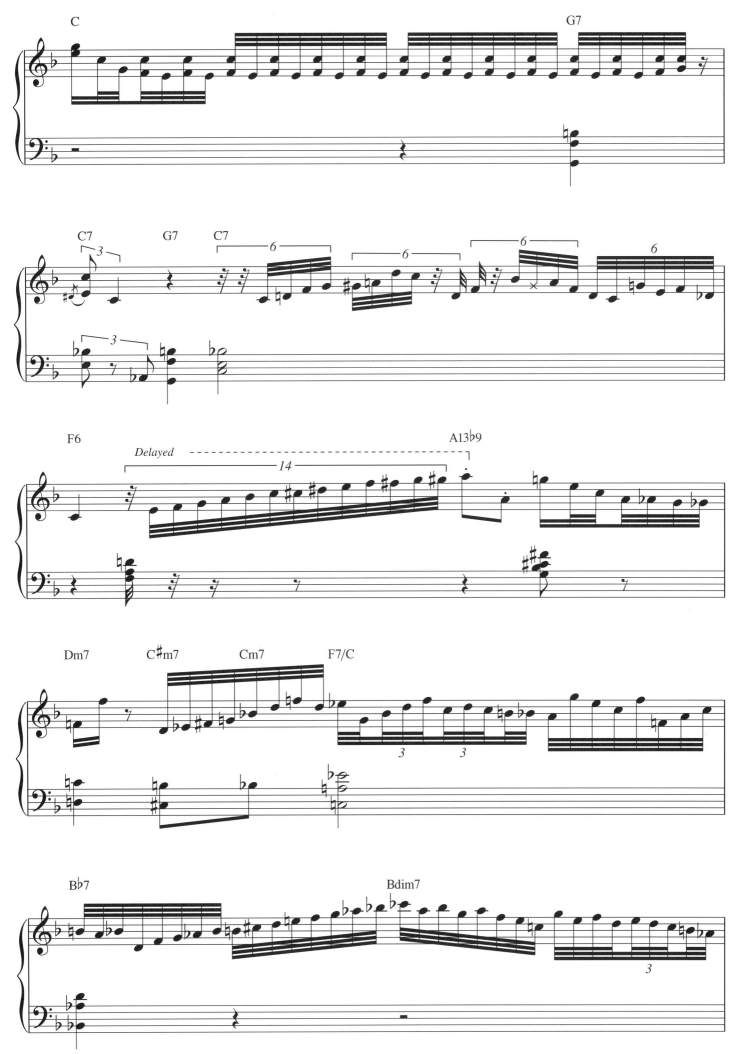

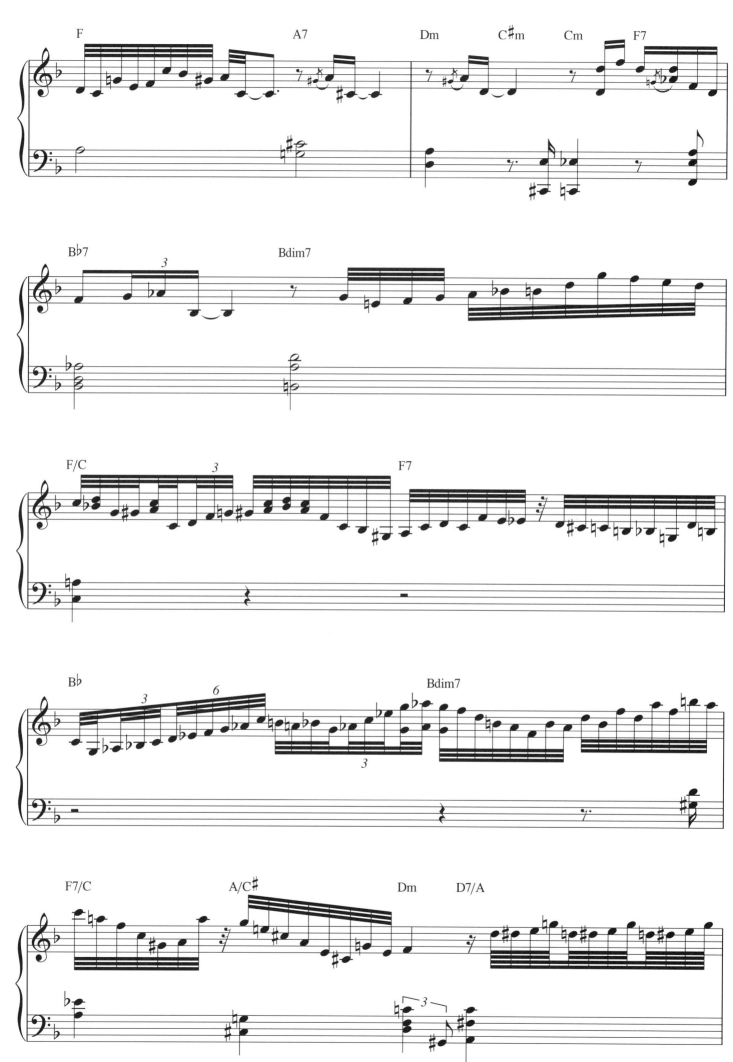

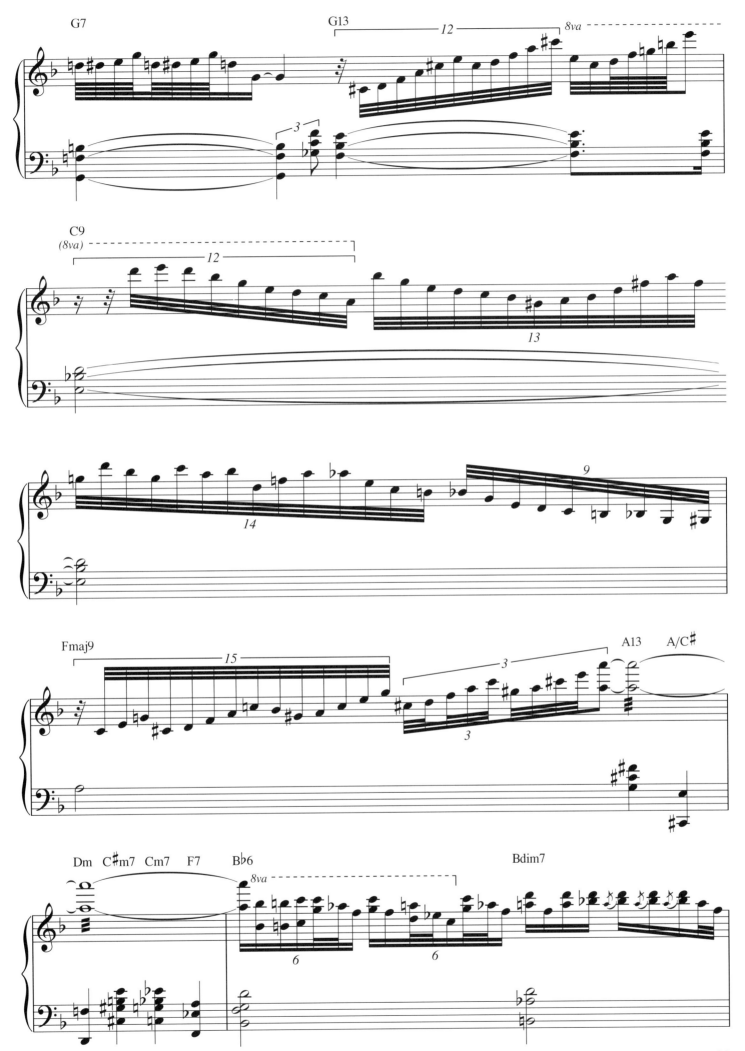

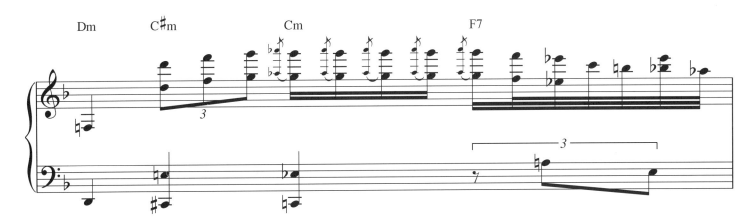

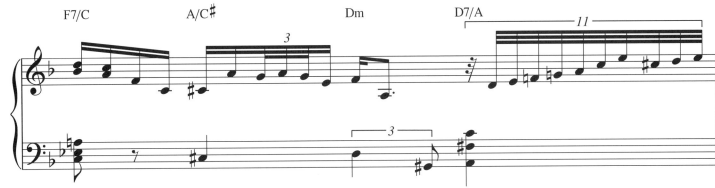

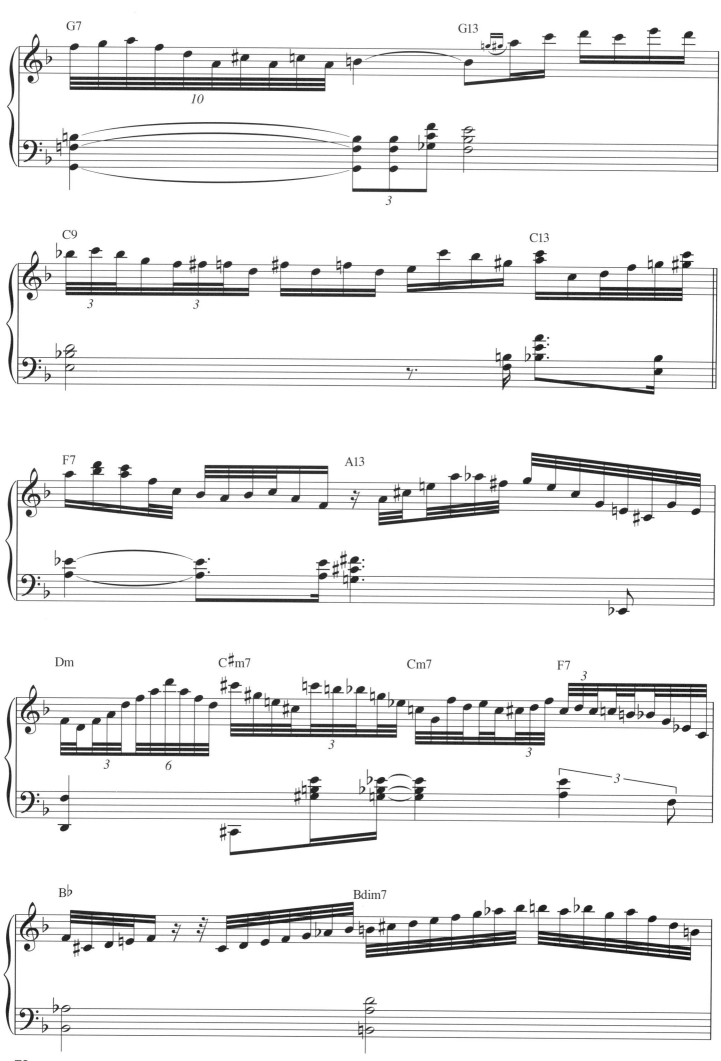

Indiana
(Back Home Again in Indiana)
Words by Ballard MacDonald
Music by James F. Hanley

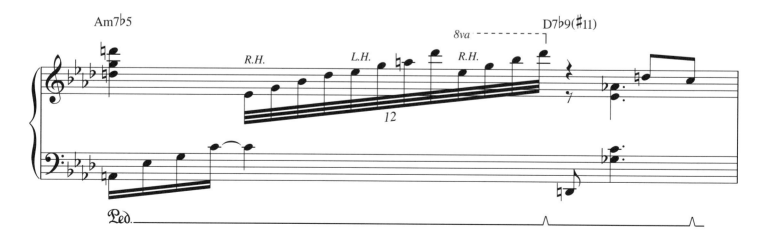

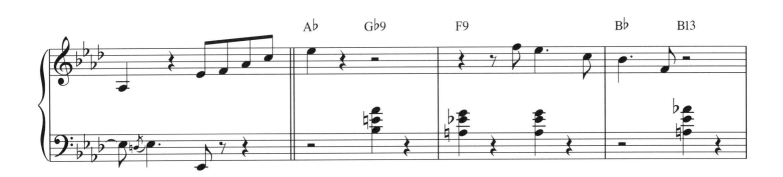

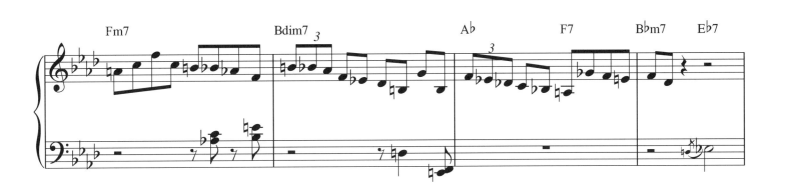

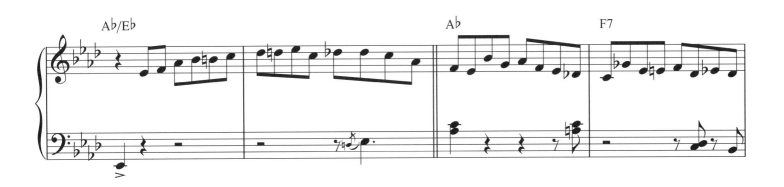

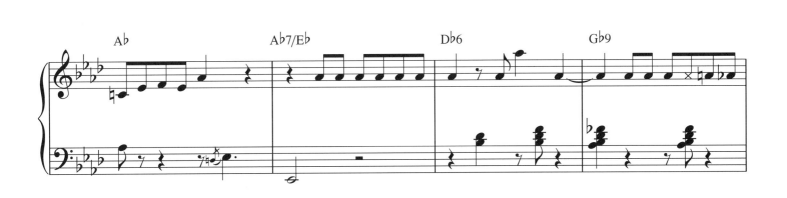

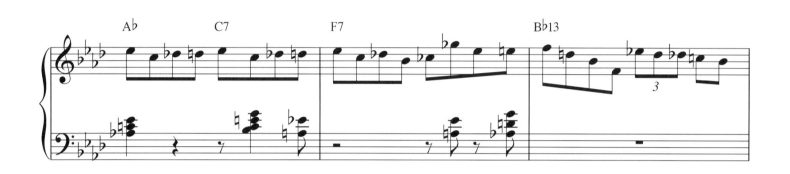

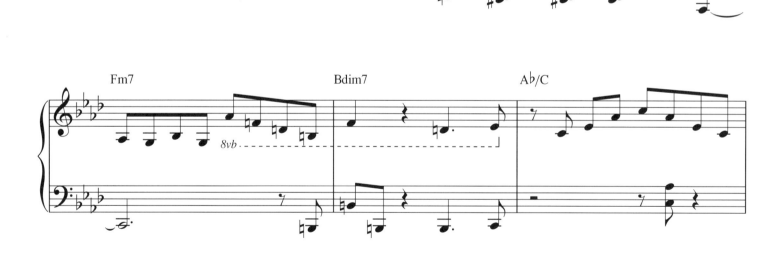

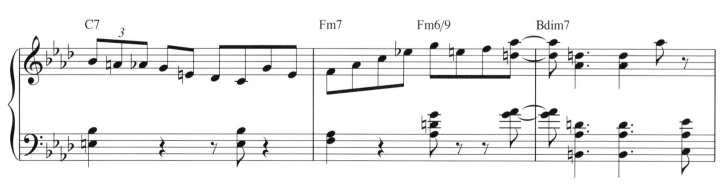

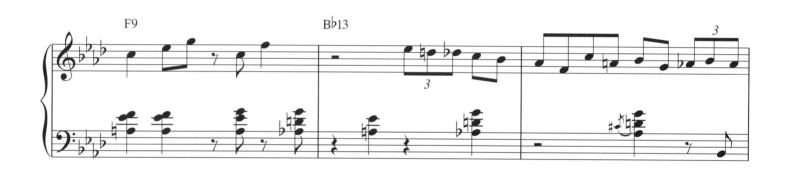

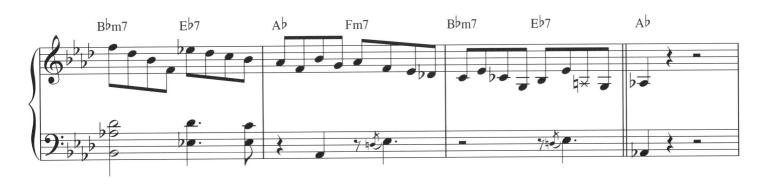

Guitar Solo

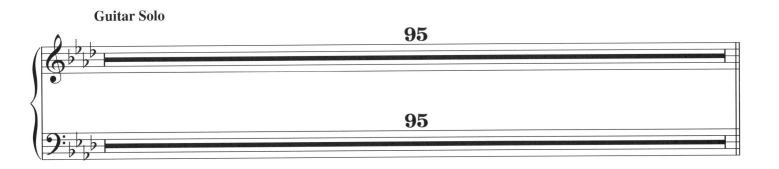

84

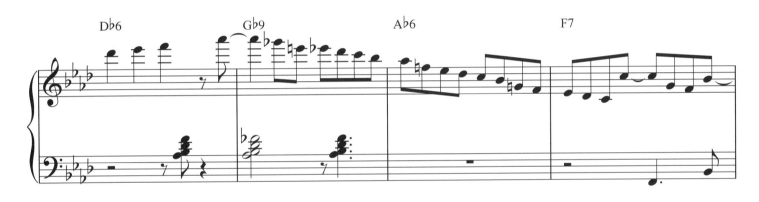

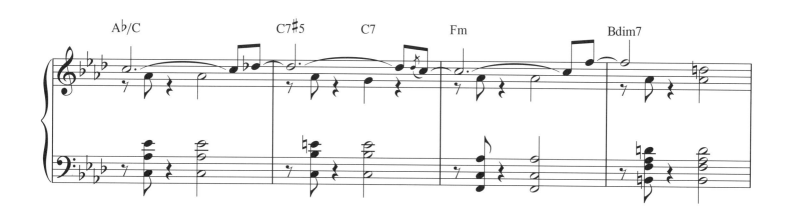

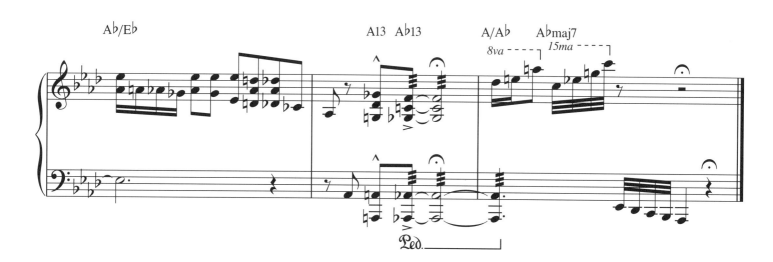

It's Only a Paper Moon

Lyric by Billy Rose and E.Y. Harburg
Music by Harold Arlen

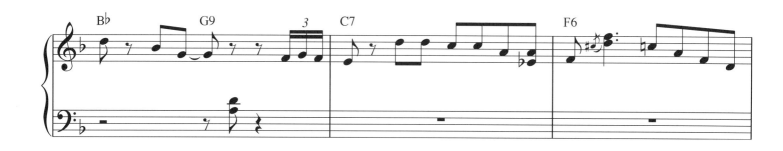

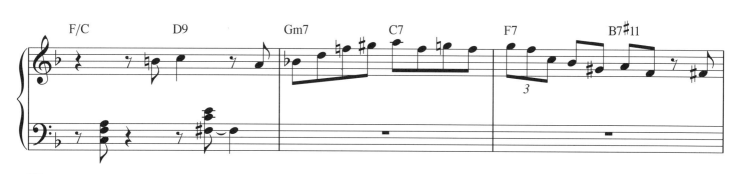

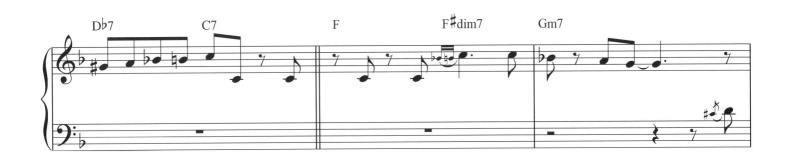

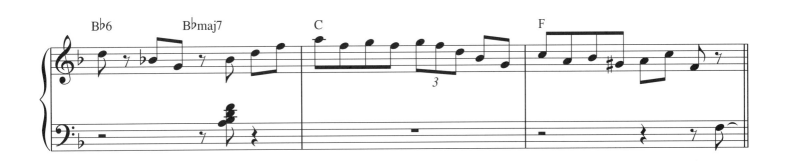

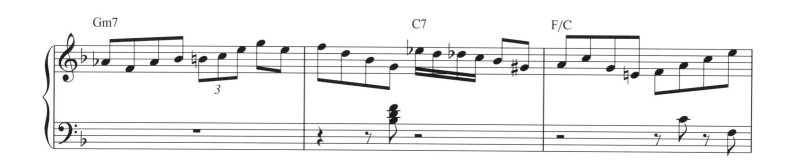

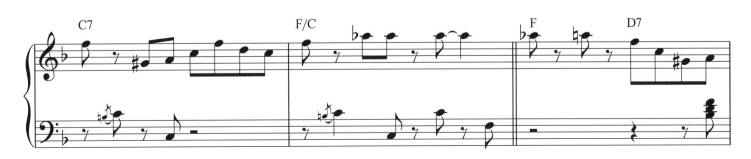

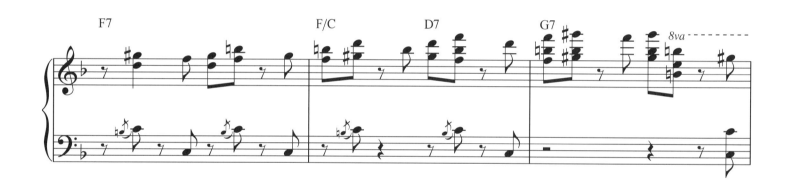

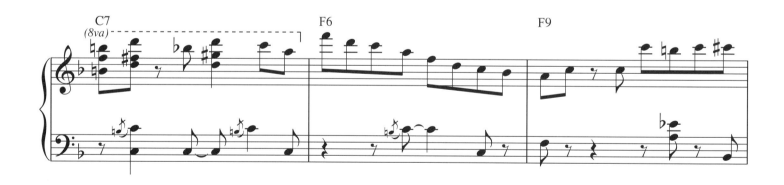

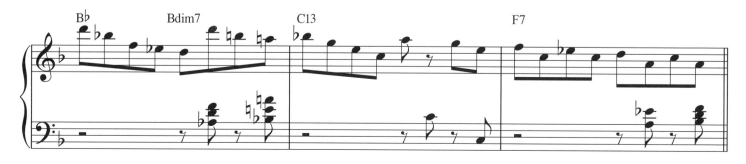

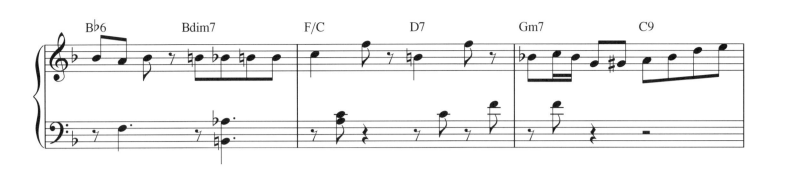

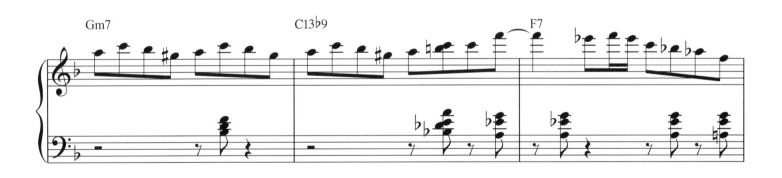

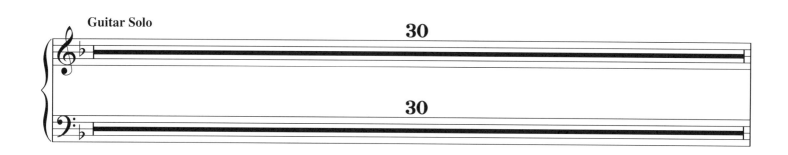

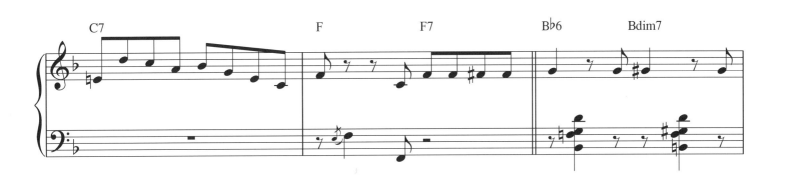

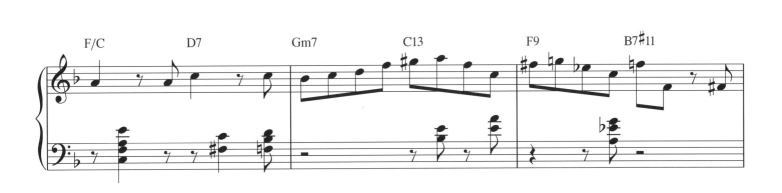

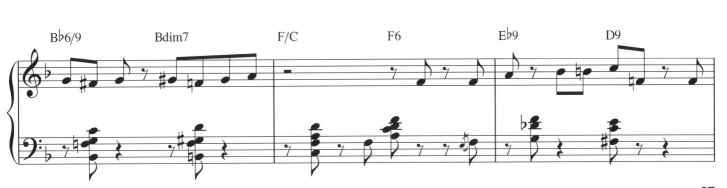

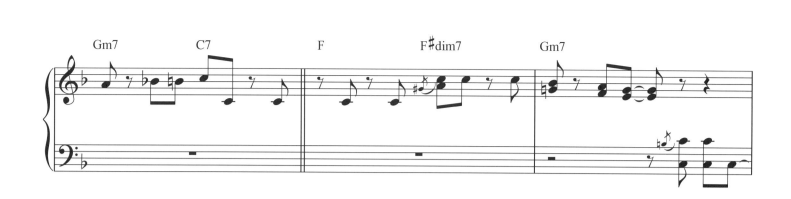

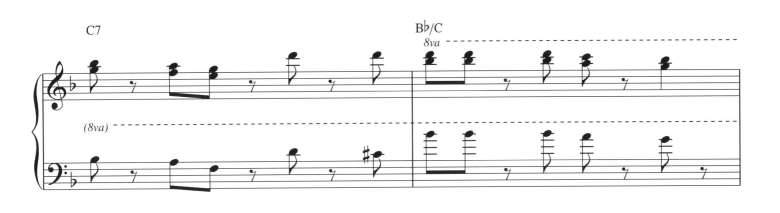

Jitterbug Waltz

Music by Thomas "Fats" Waller

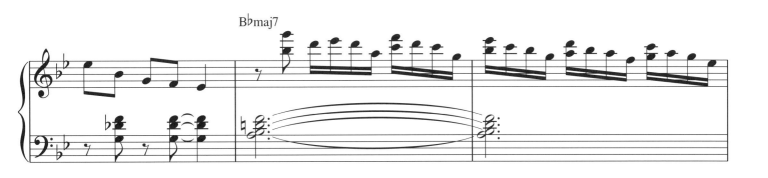

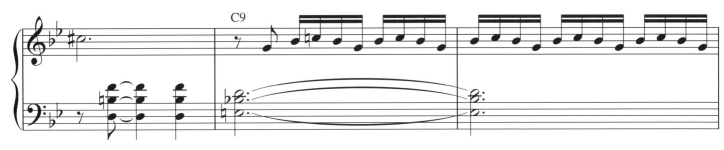

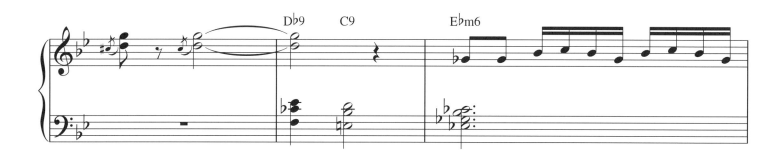

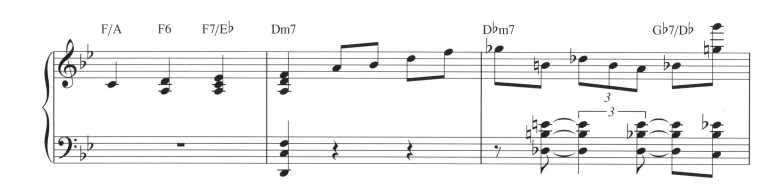

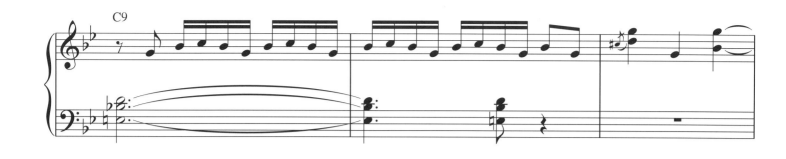

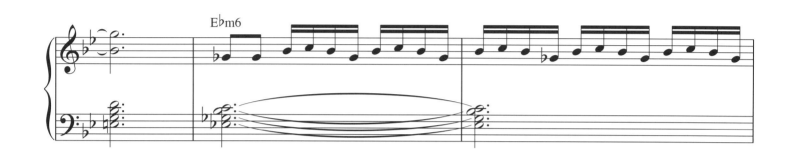

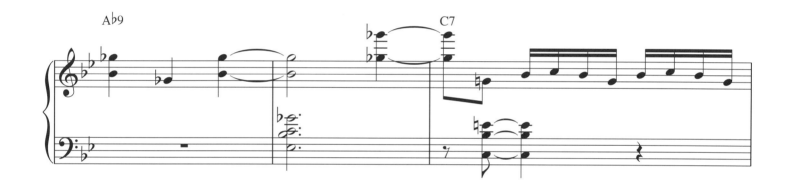

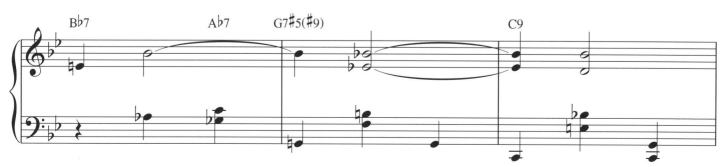

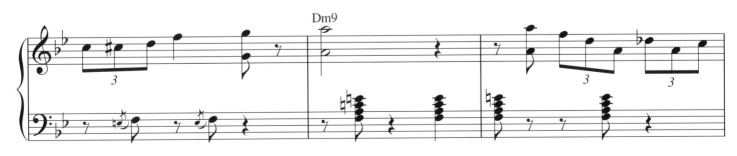

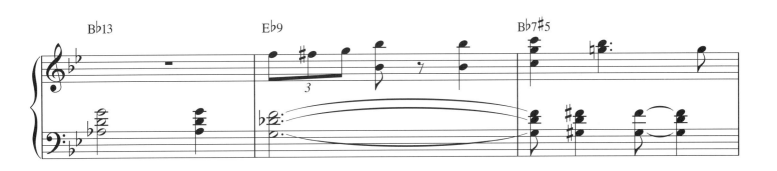

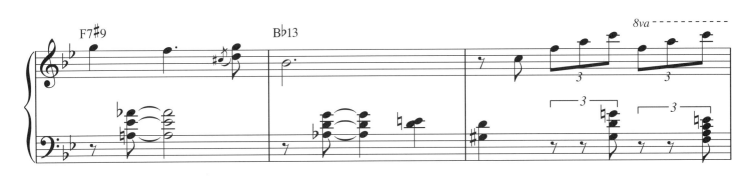

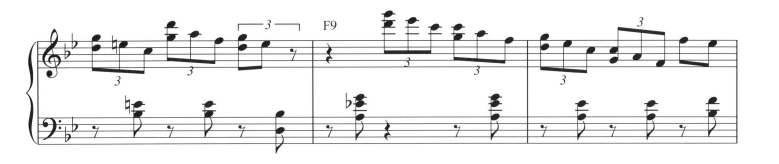

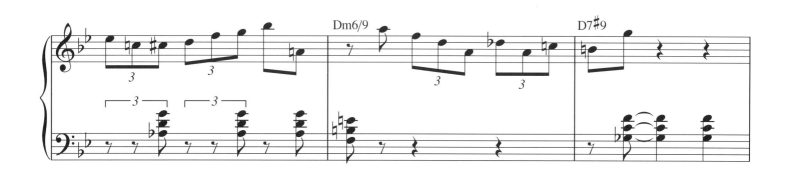

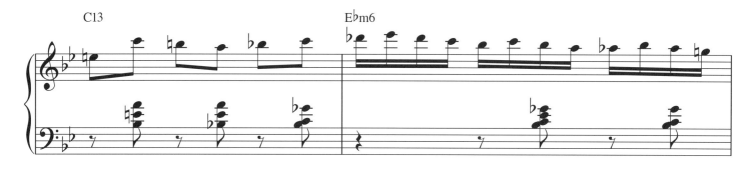

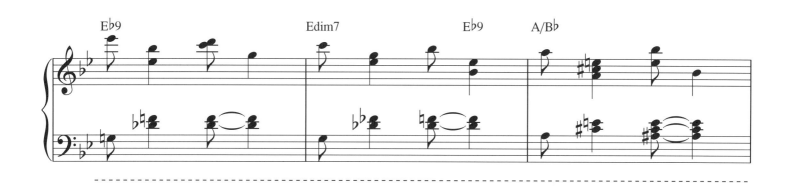

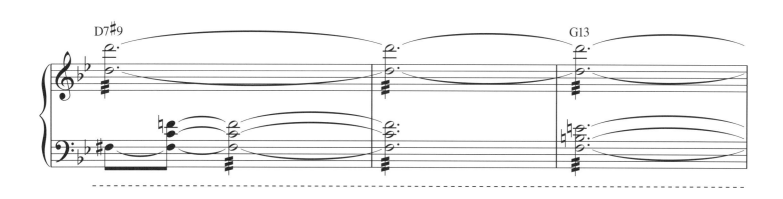

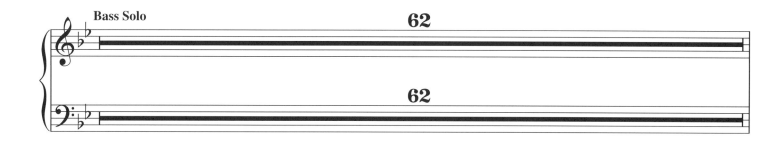

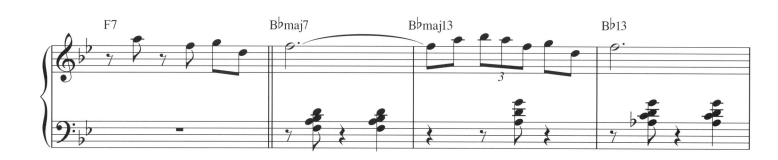

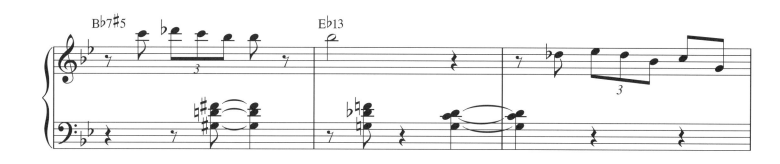

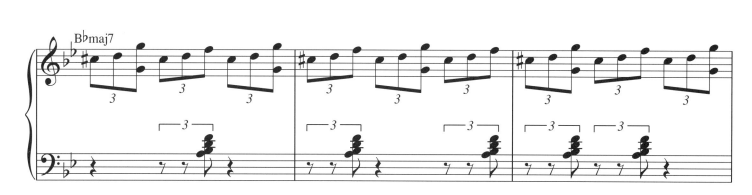

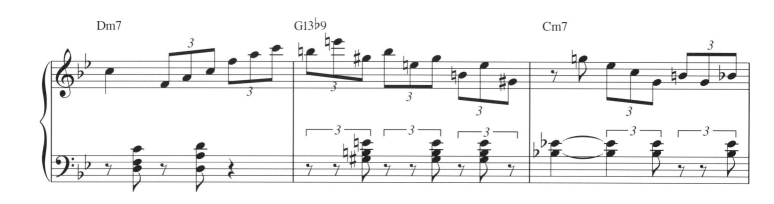

116

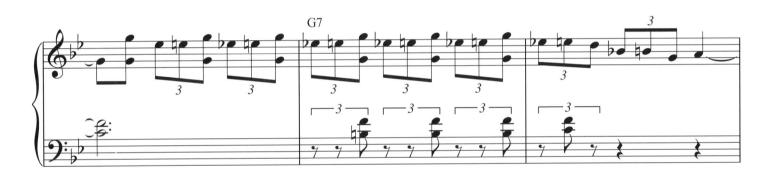

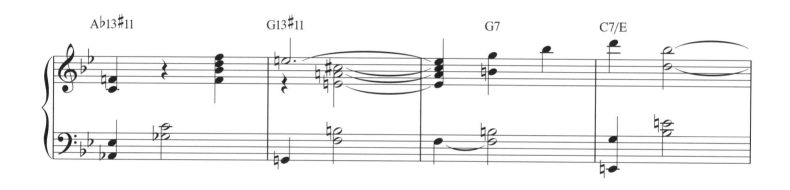

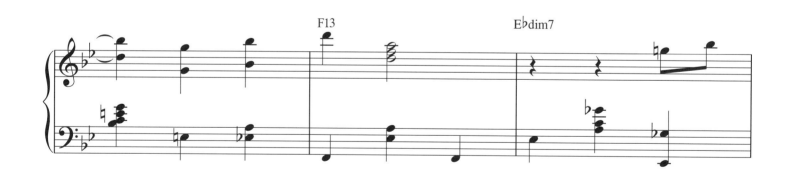

119

Laura

Music by David Raksin
Lyric by Johnny Mercer

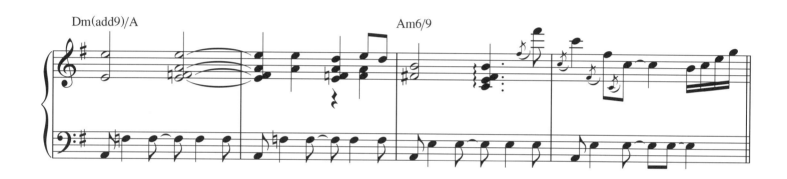

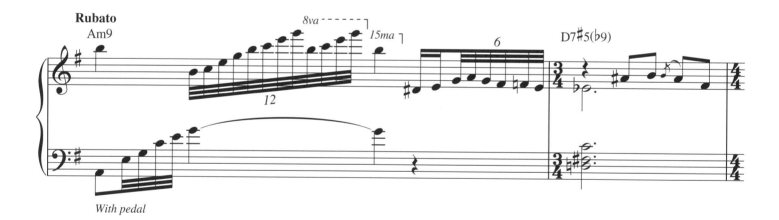

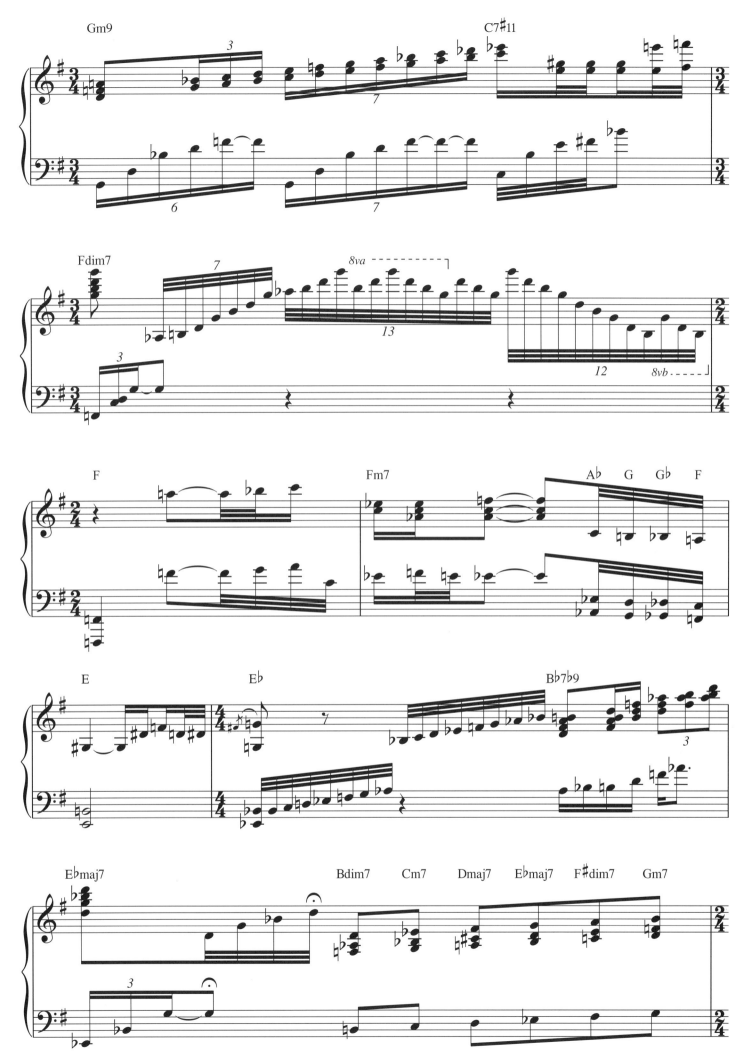

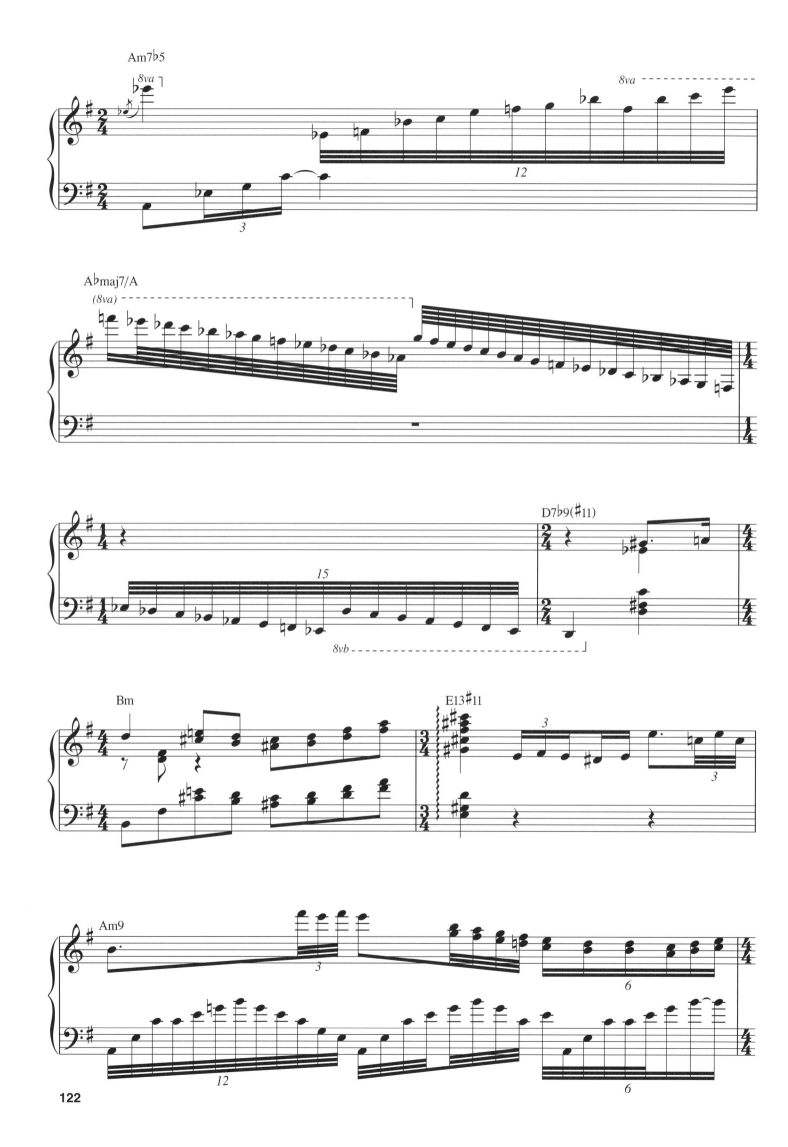

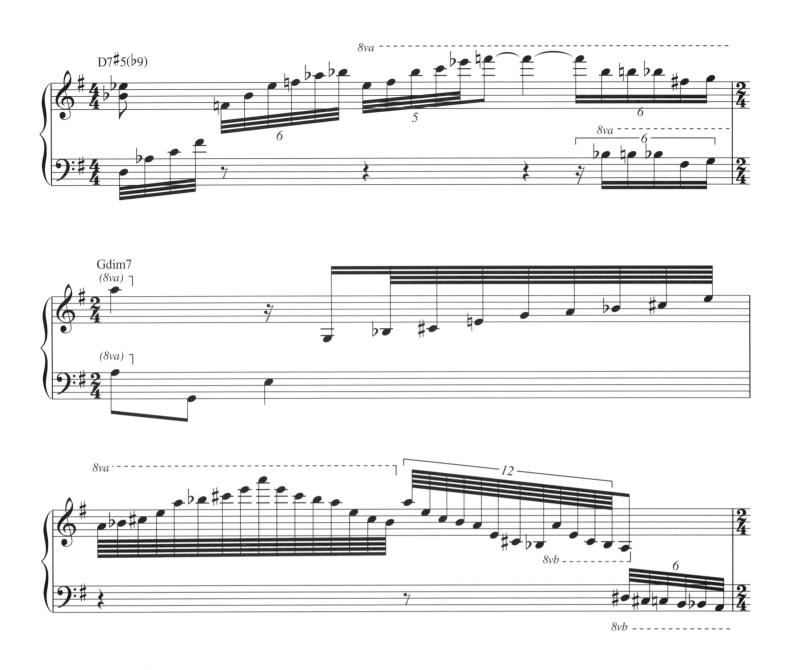

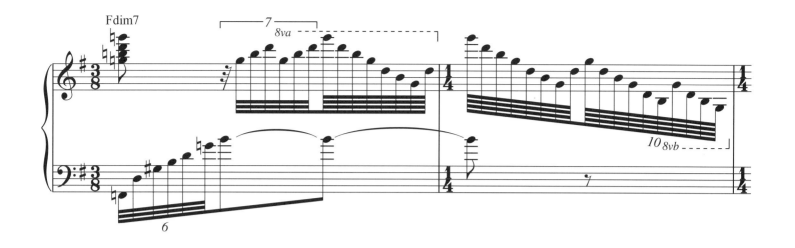

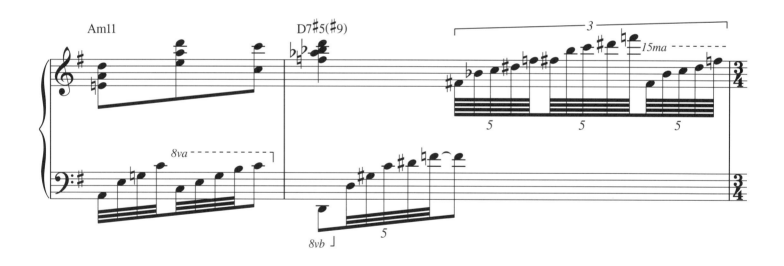

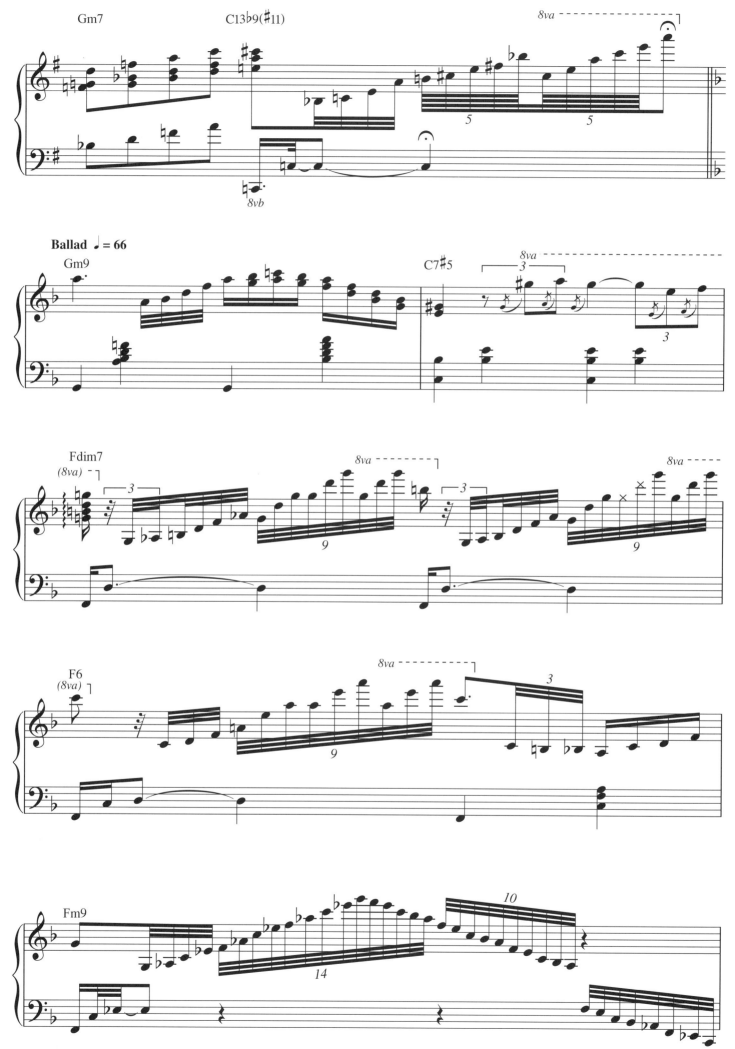

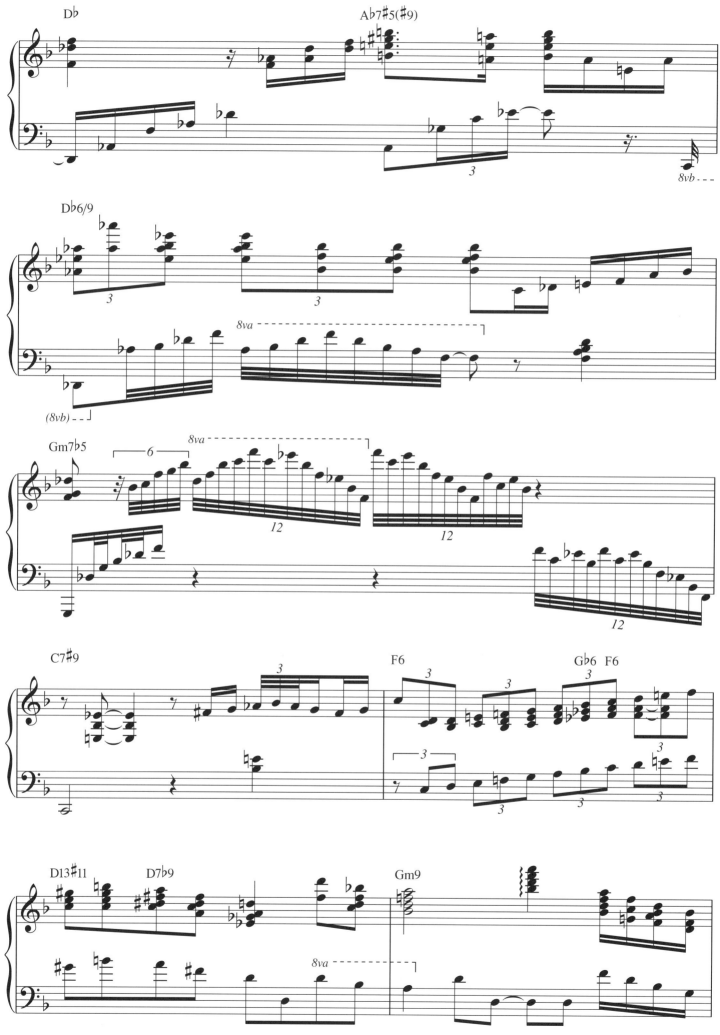

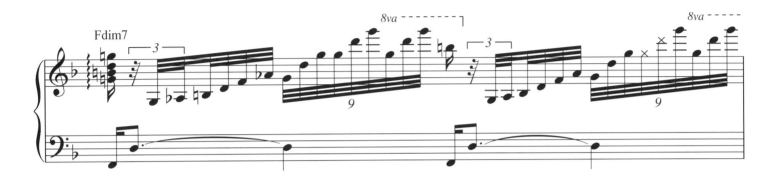

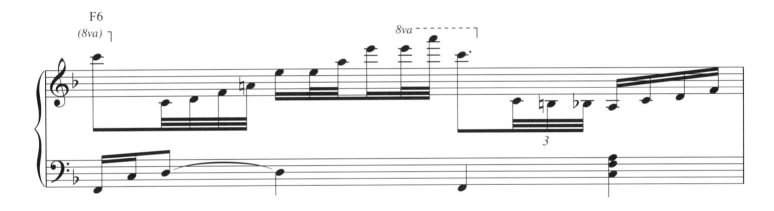

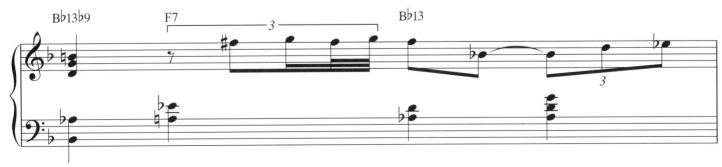

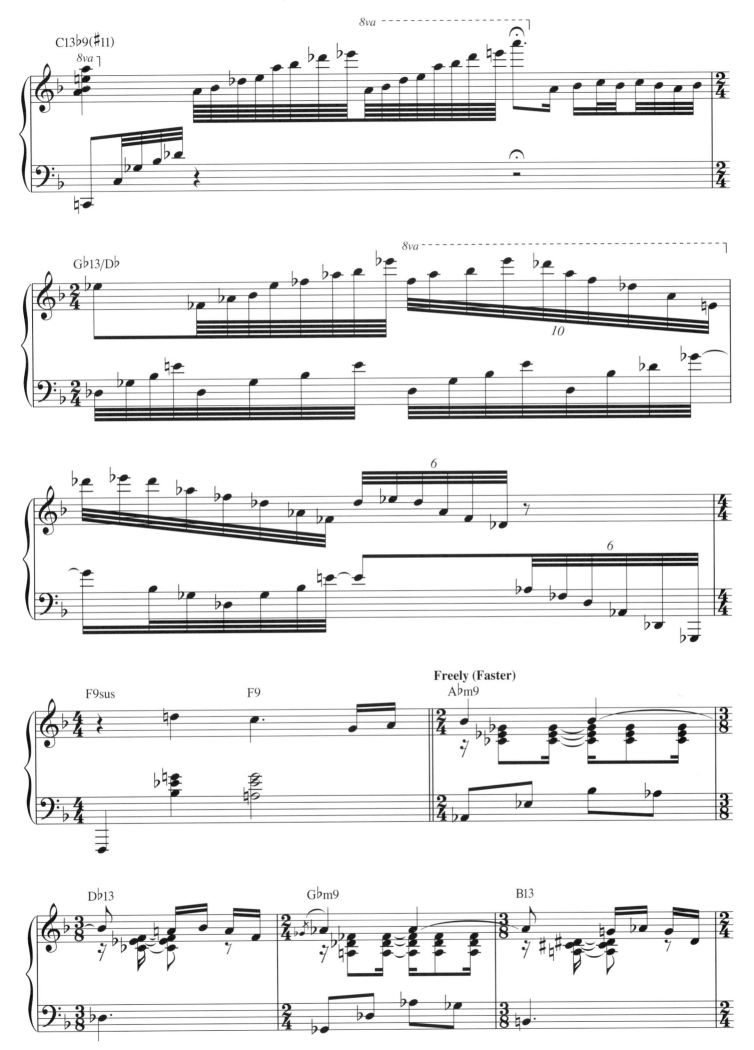

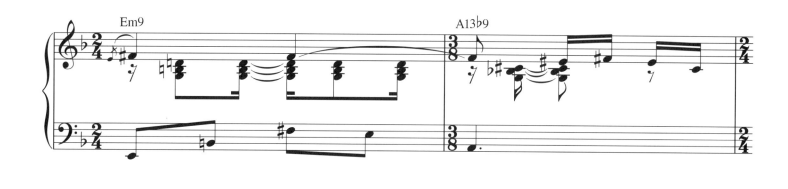

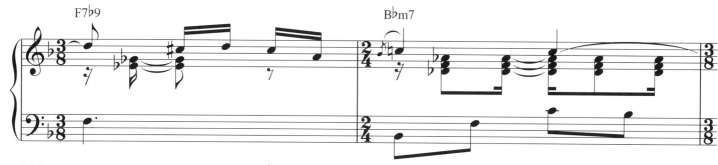

138

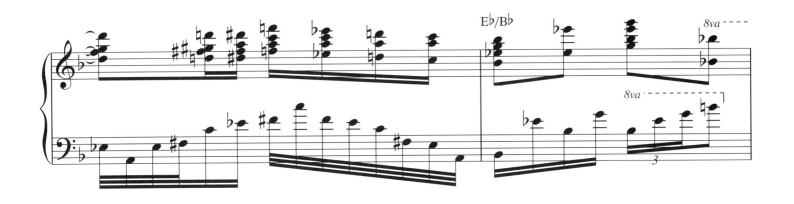

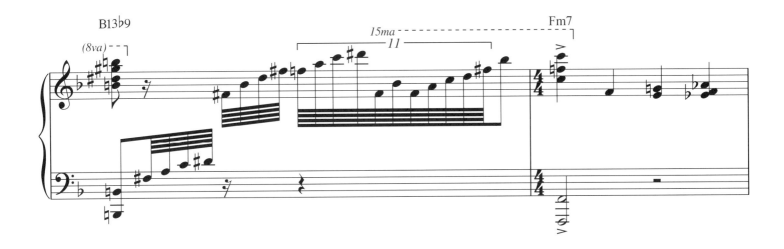

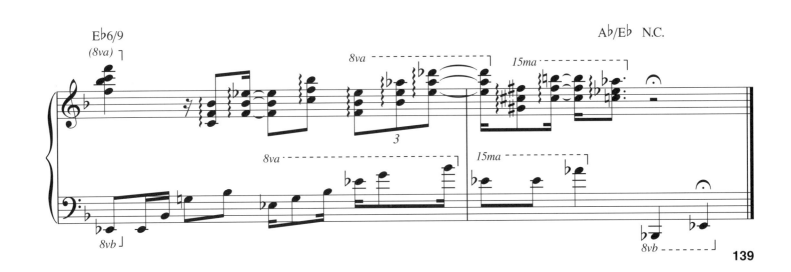

Lover
from the Paramount Picture LOVE ME TONIGHT

Words by Lorenz Hart
Music by Richard Rodgers

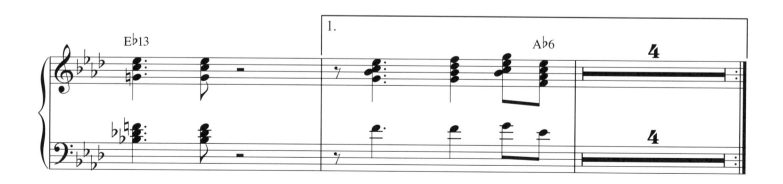

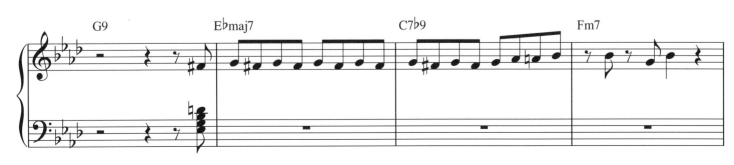

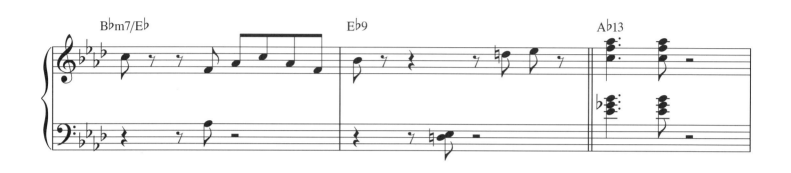

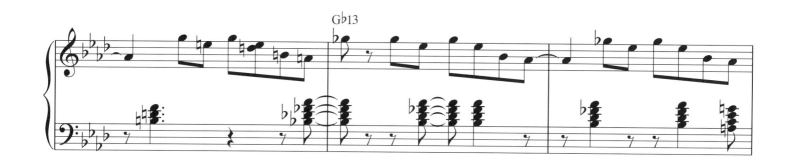

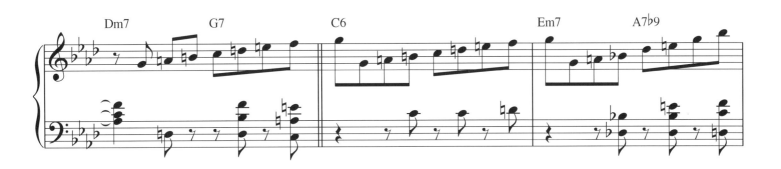

146

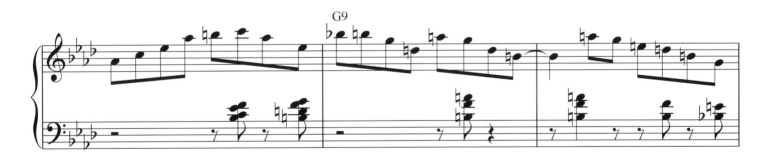

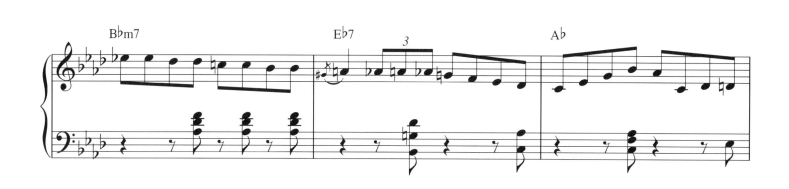

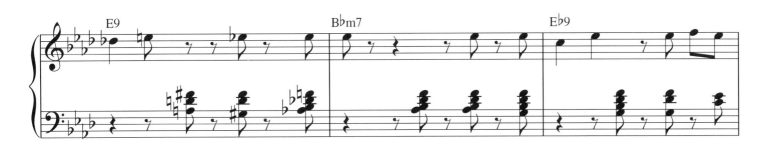

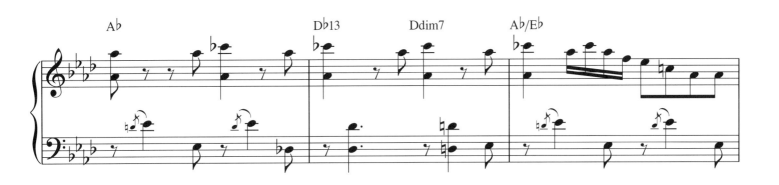

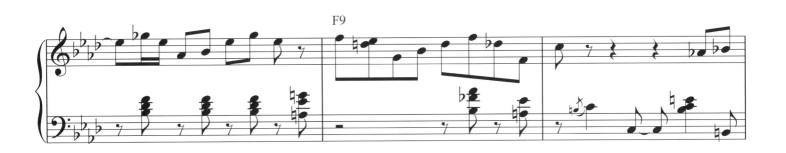

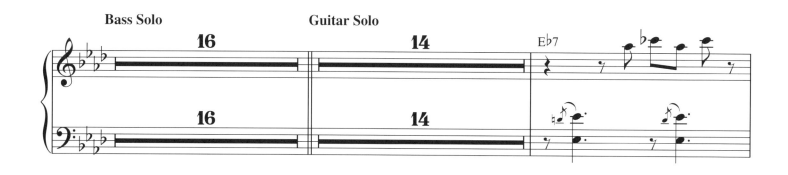

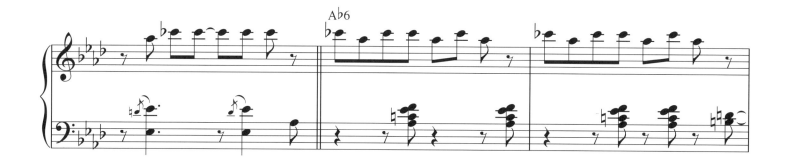

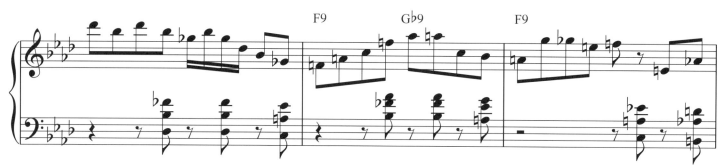

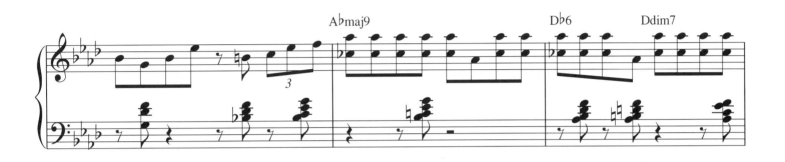

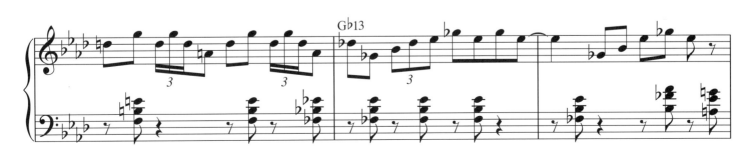

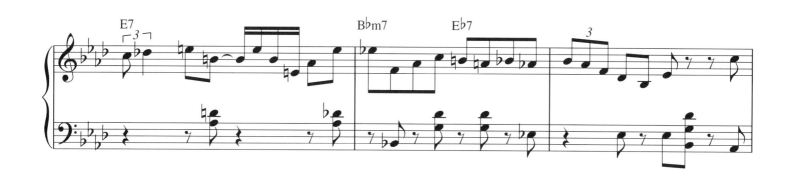

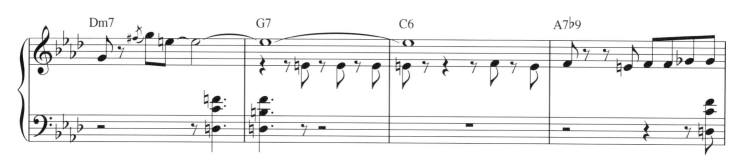

154

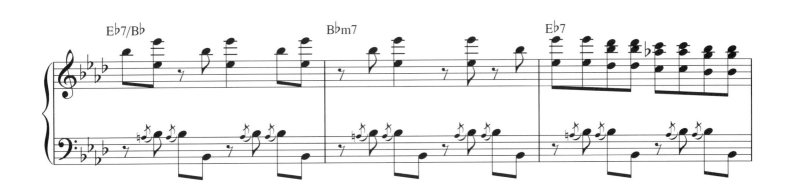

Misty

Music by Erroll Garner

158

Bass Solo and cadenza

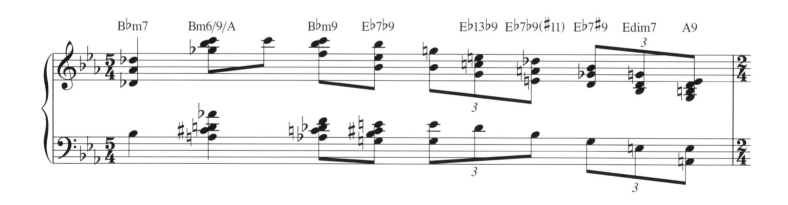

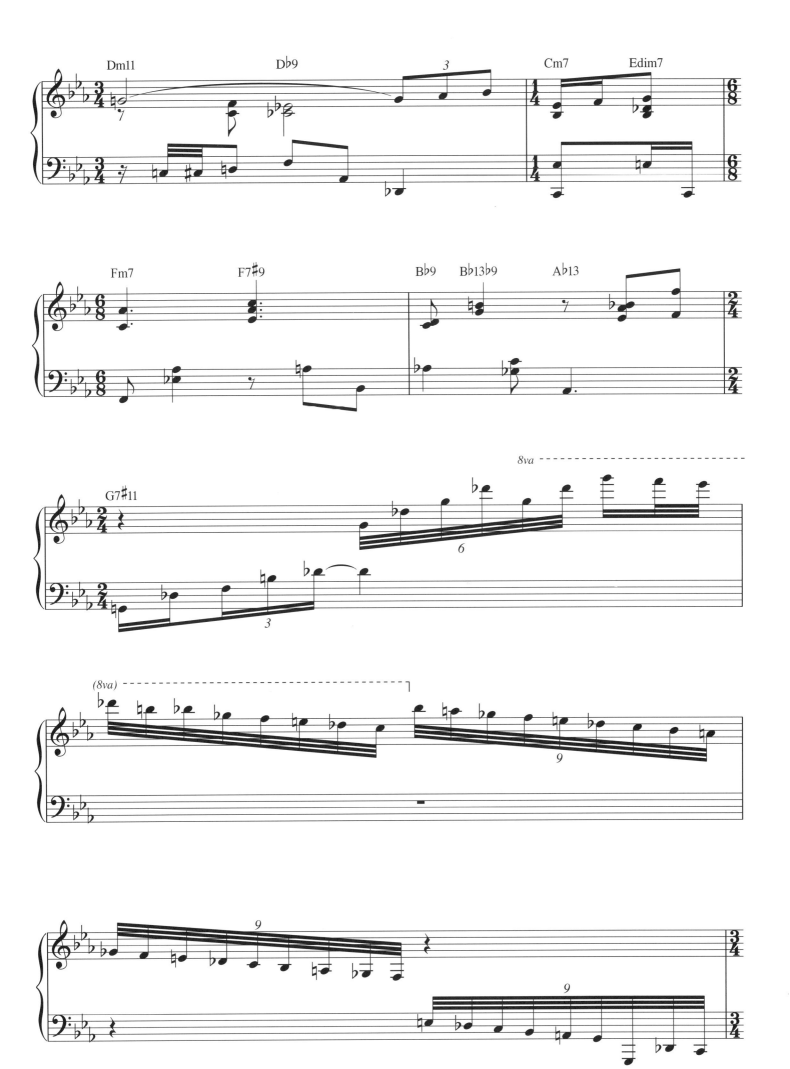

Ballad tempo ♩ = 56

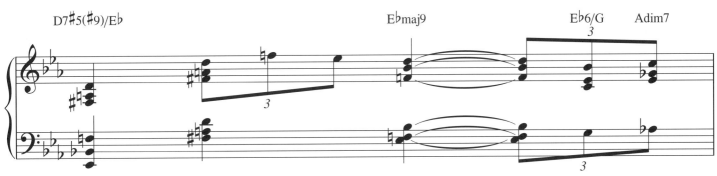

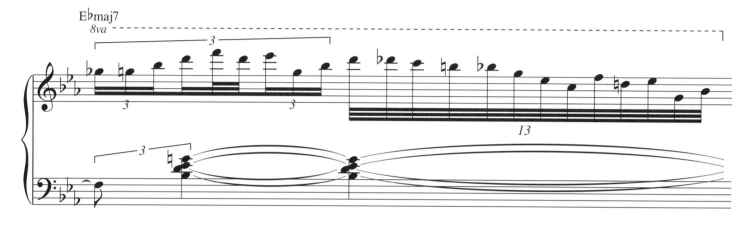

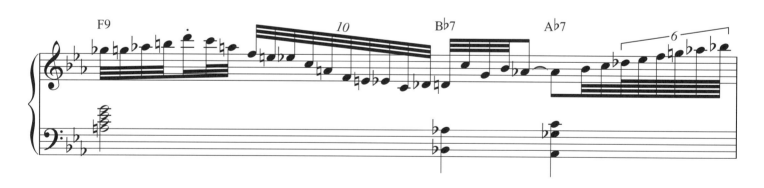

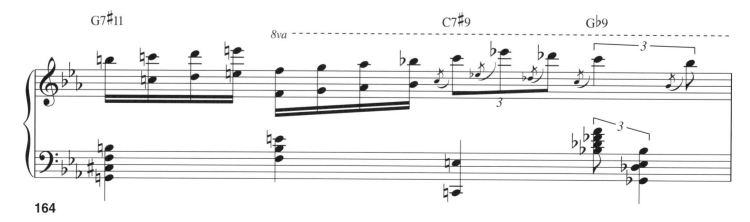

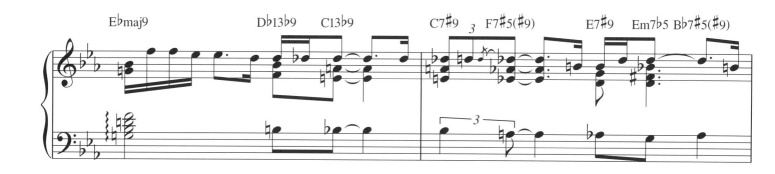

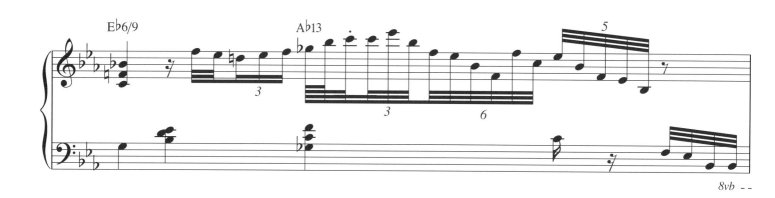

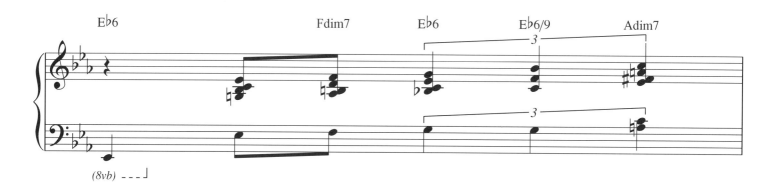

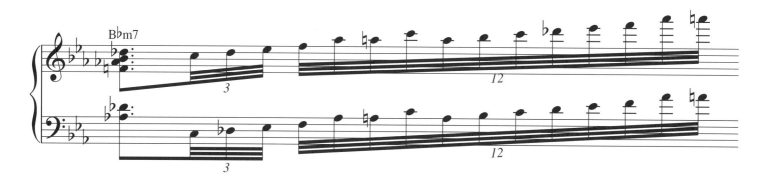

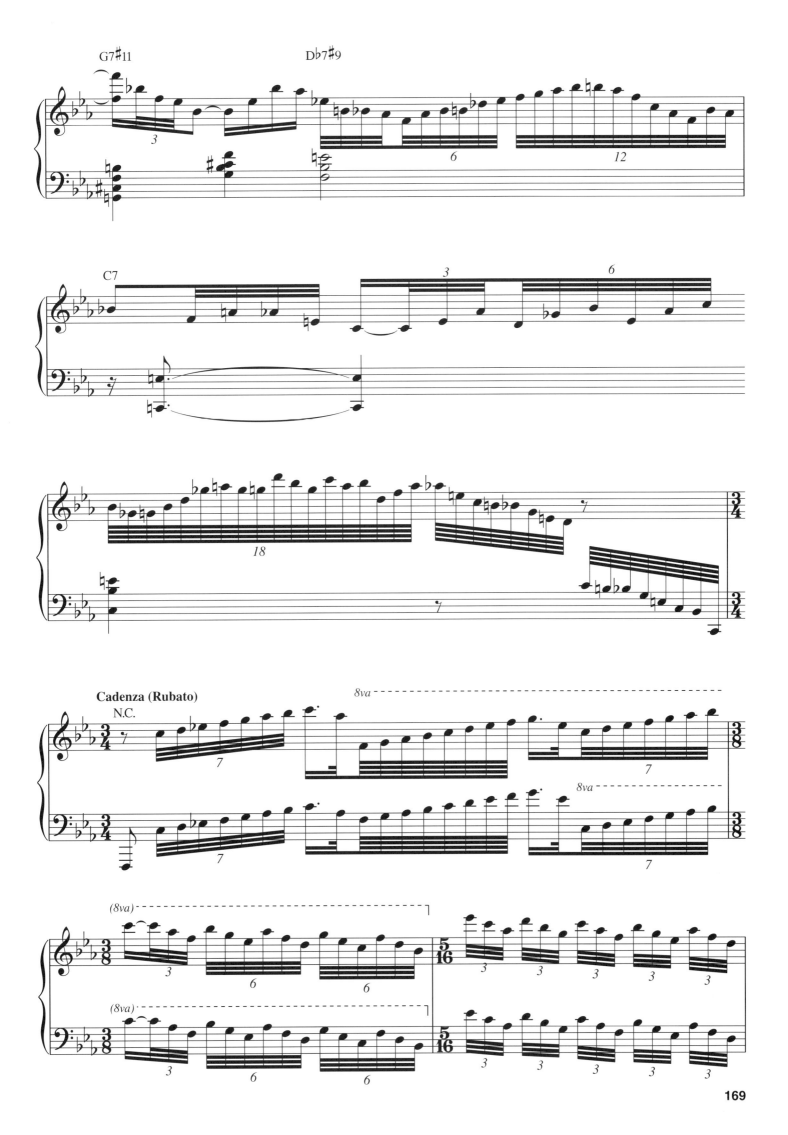

169

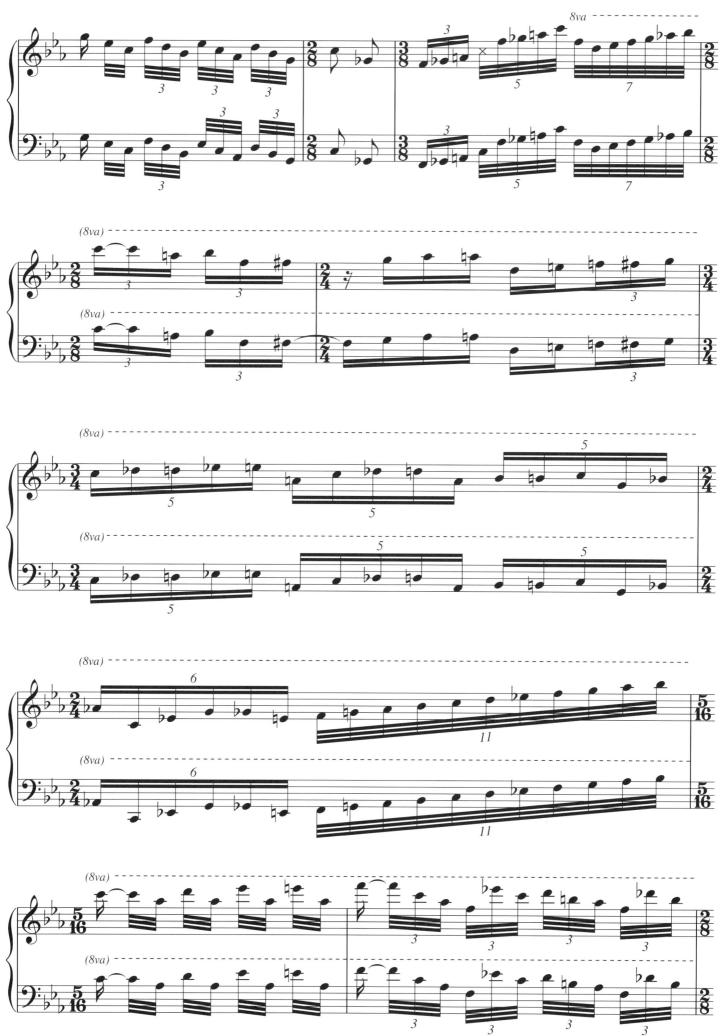

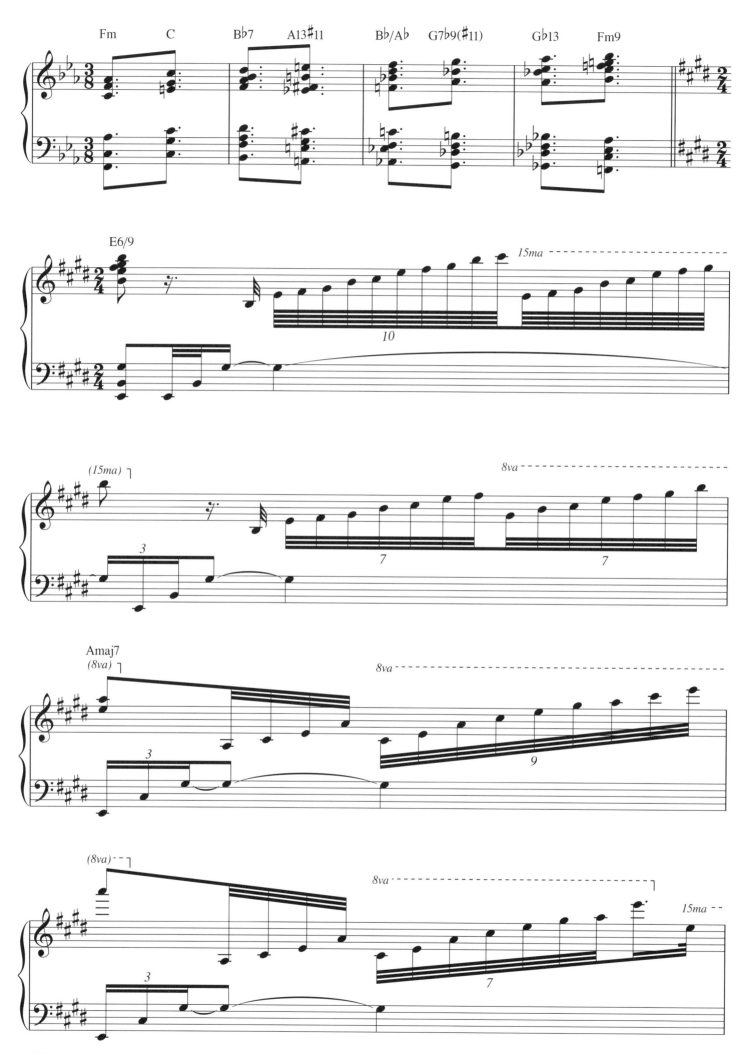

Night and Day

from GAY DIVORCE

Words and Music by Cole Porter

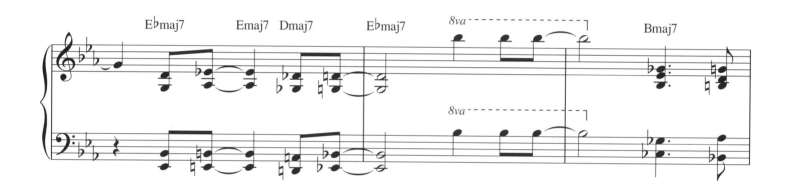

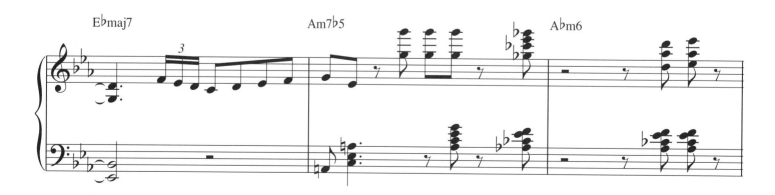

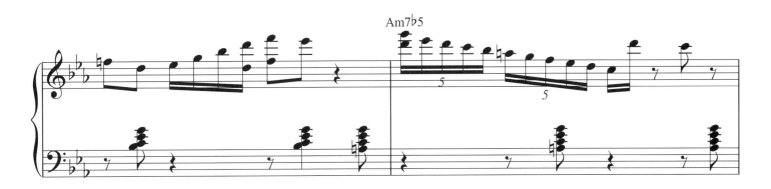

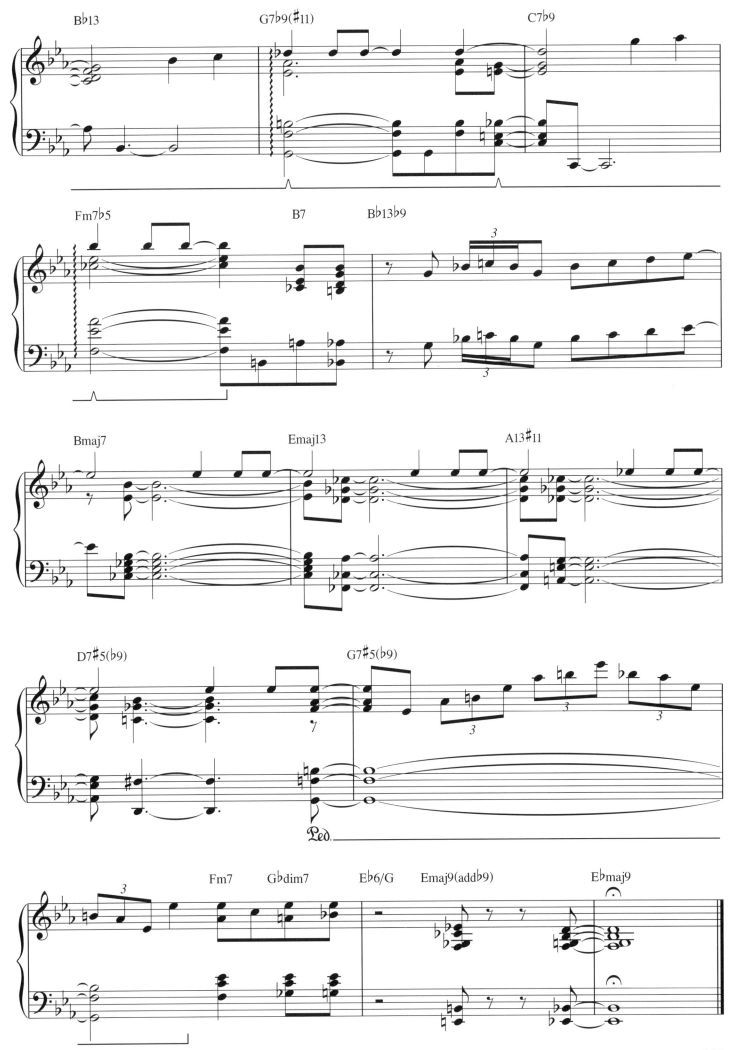

Quiet Nights of Quiet Stars

(Corcovado)

English Words by Gene Lees
Original Words and Music by Antonio Carlos Jobim

Bright Bossa Nova ♩ = 170

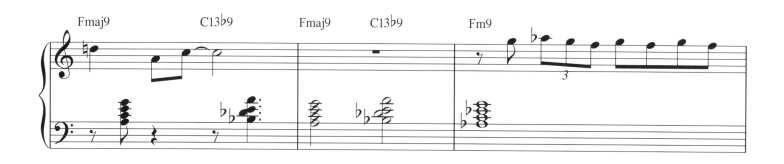

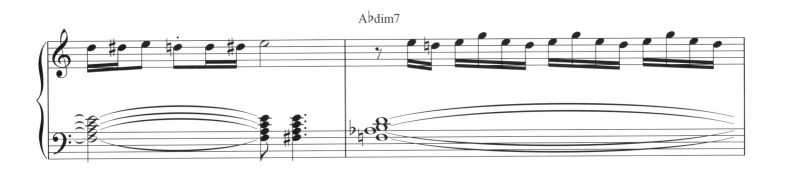

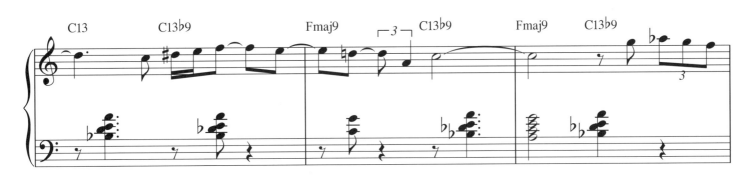

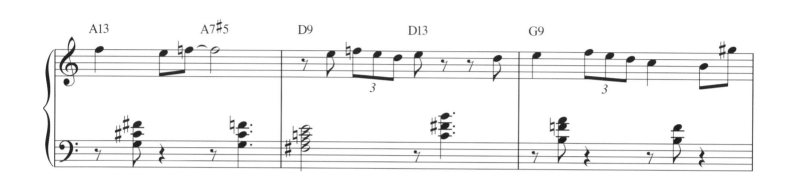

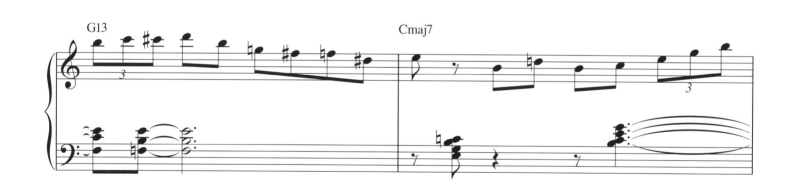

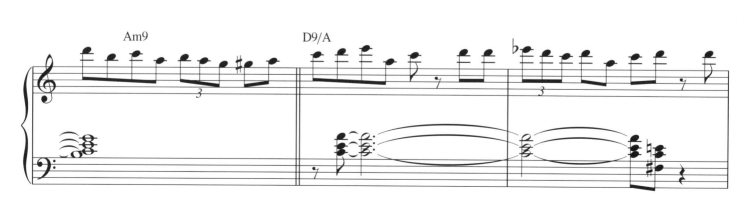

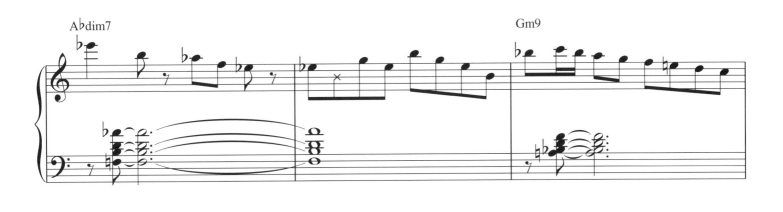

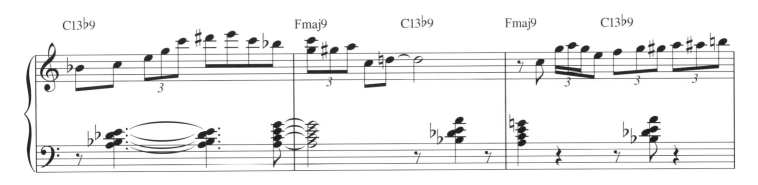

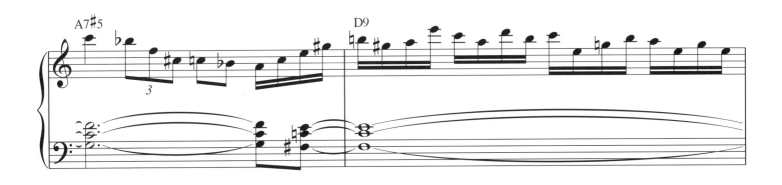

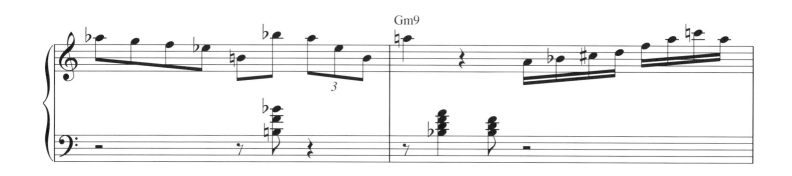

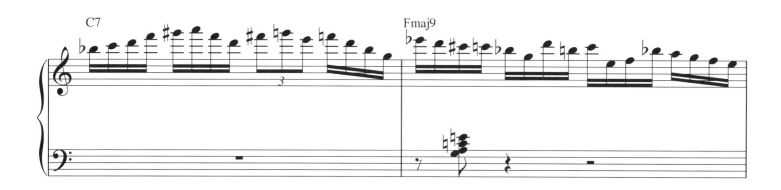

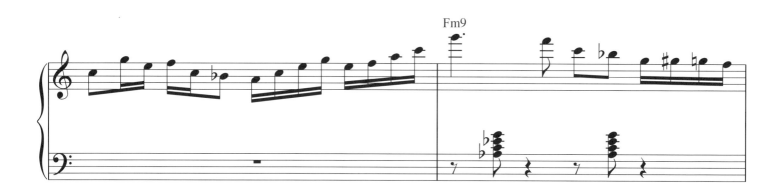

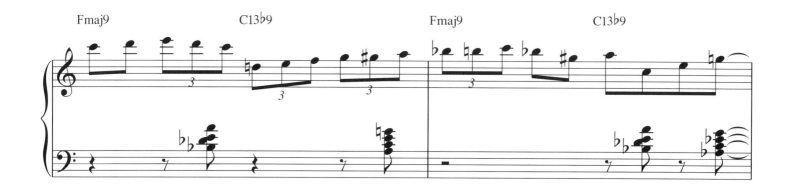

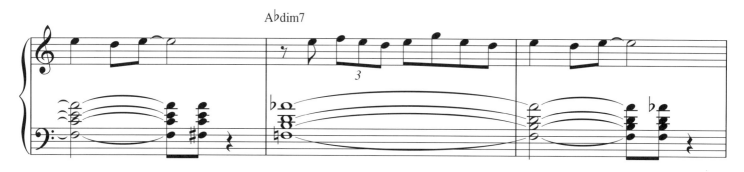

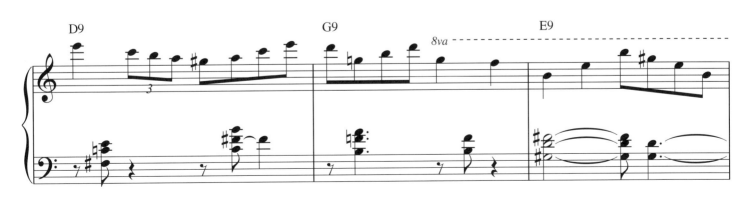

189

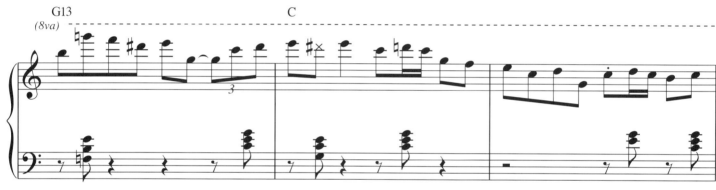

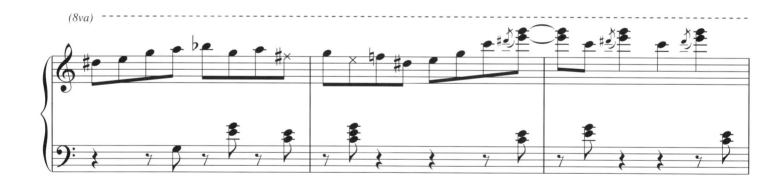

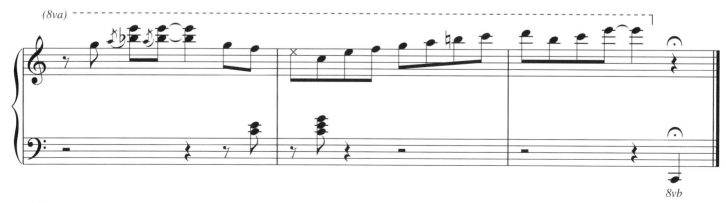

Tangerine

from the Paramount Picture THE FLEET'S IN

Words by Johnny Mercer
Music by Victor Schertzinger

193

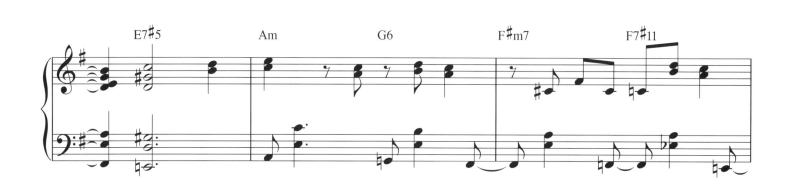

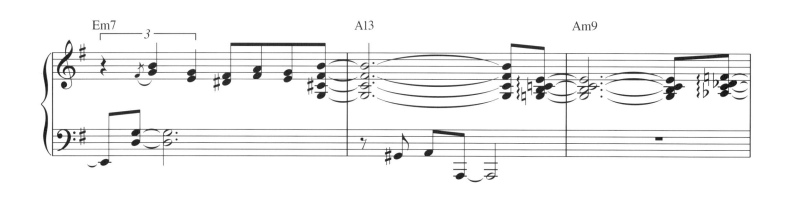

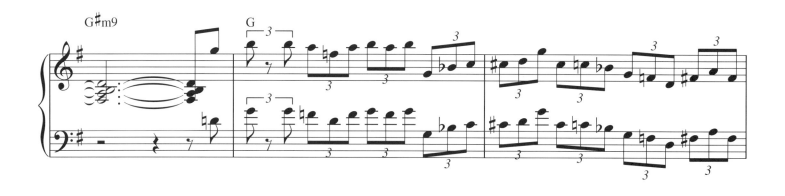

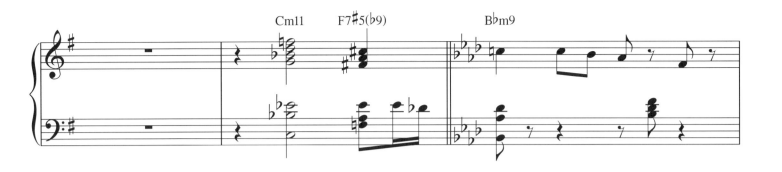

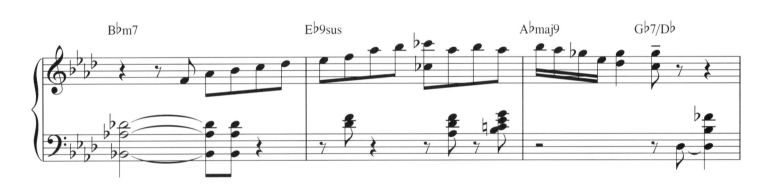

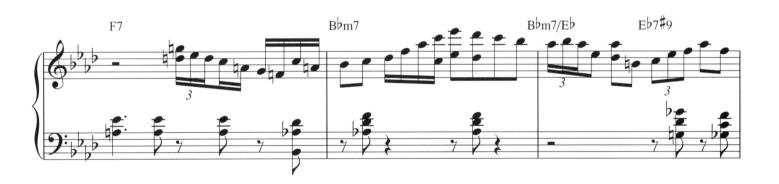

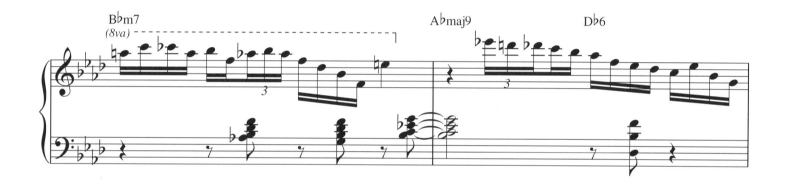

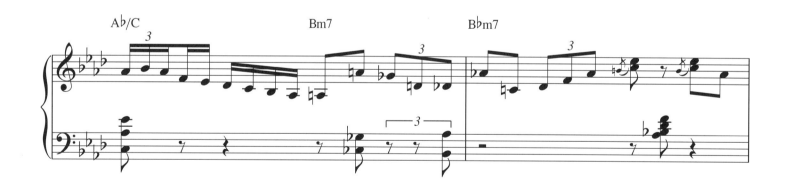

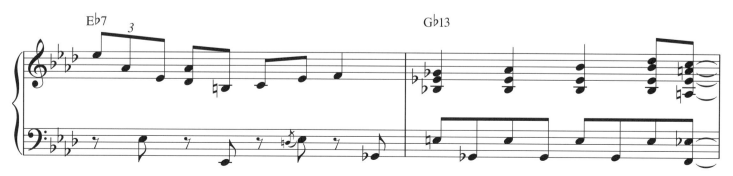

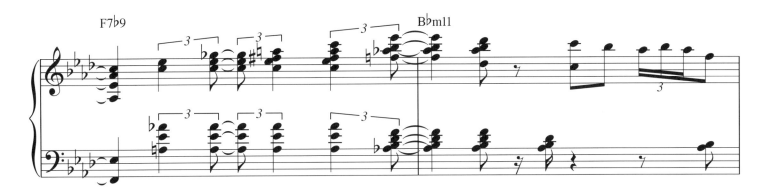

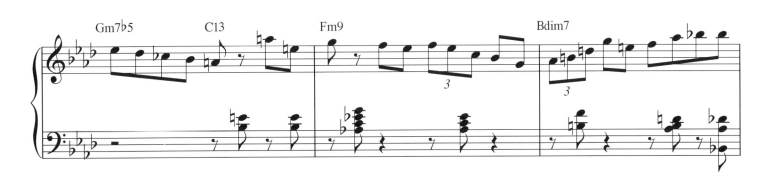

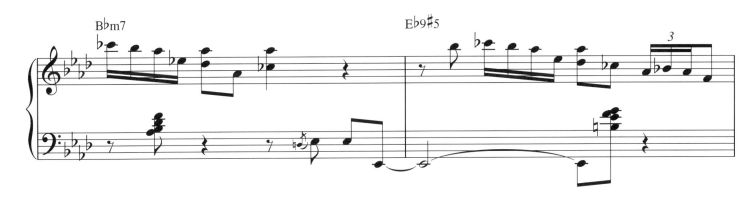

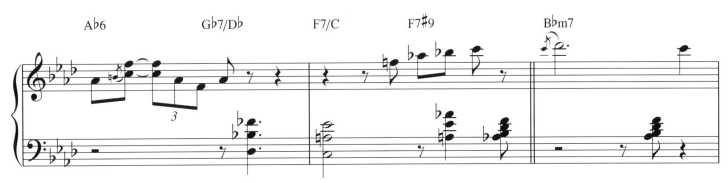

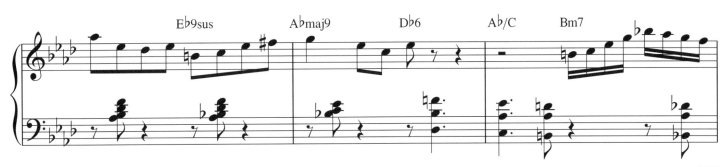

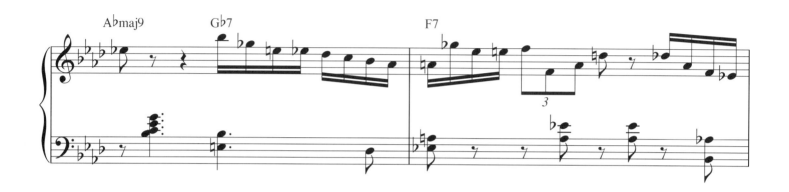

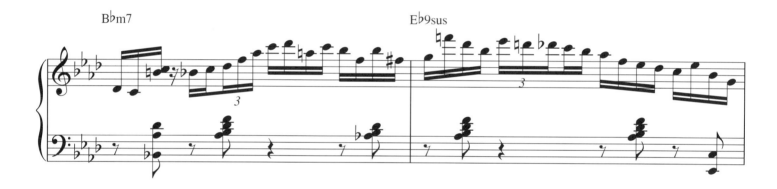

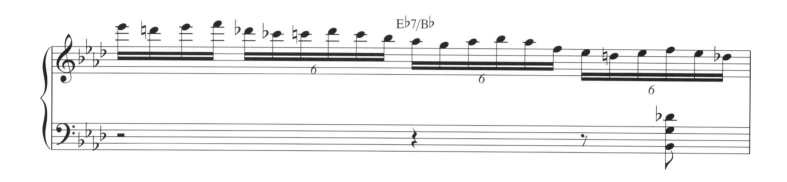

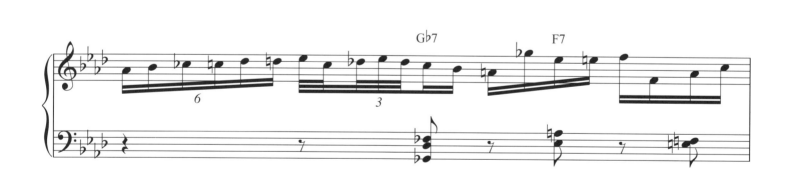

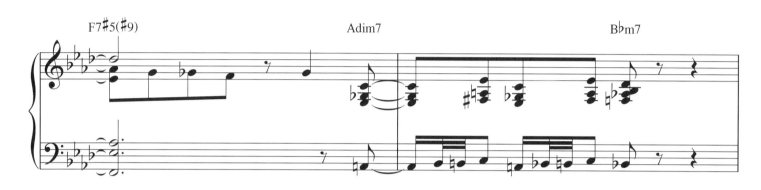

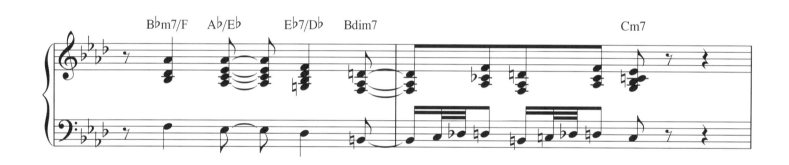

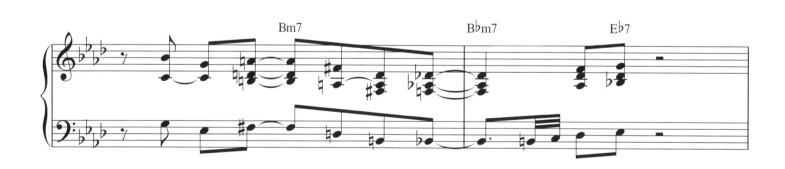

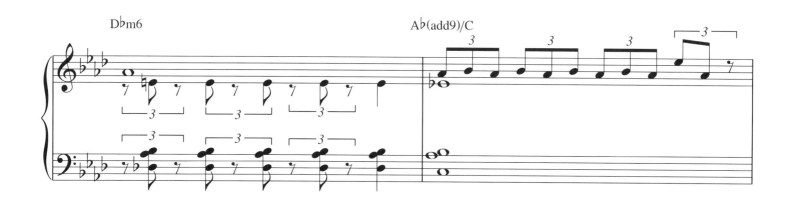

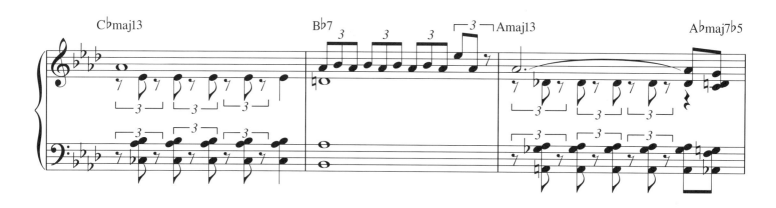

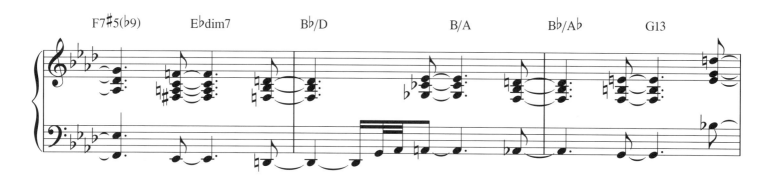

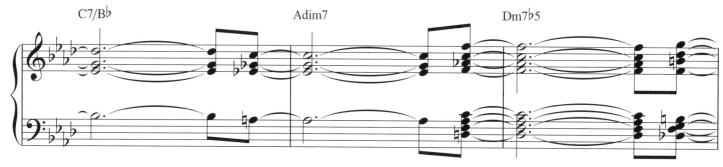

Teach Me Tonight

Words by Sammy Cahn
Music by Gene DePaul

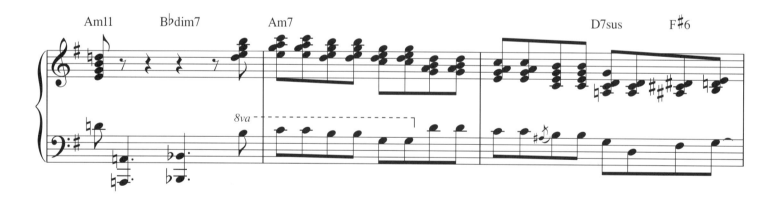

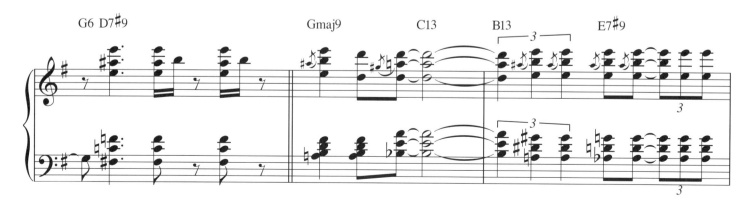

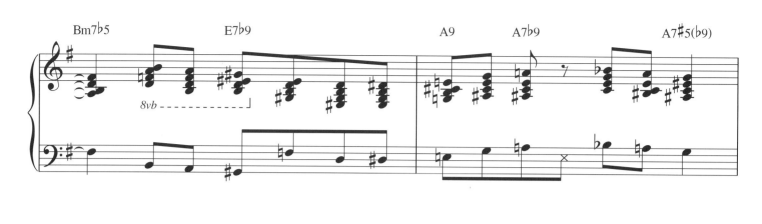

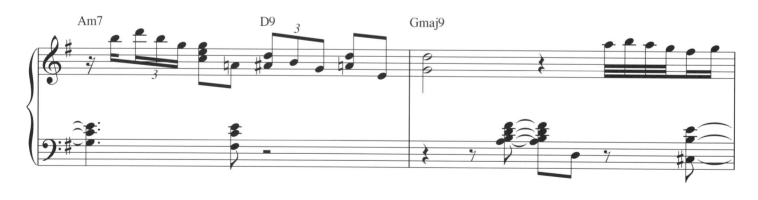

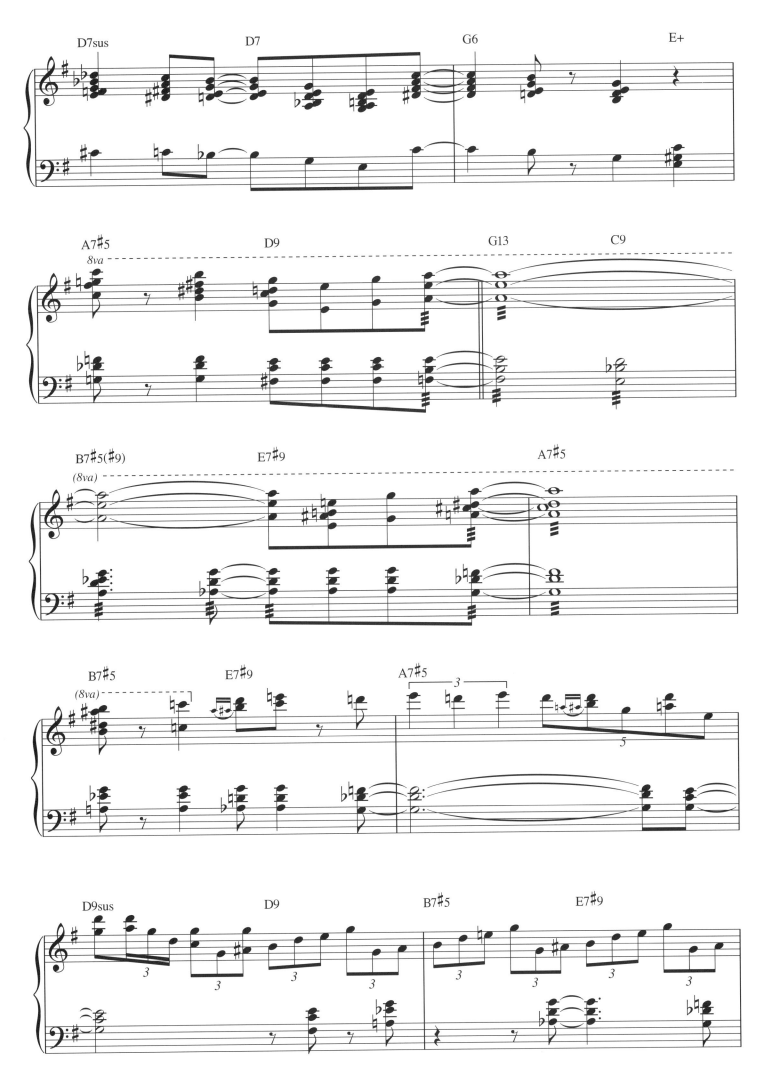

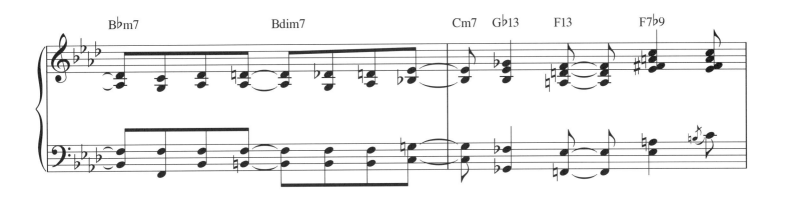

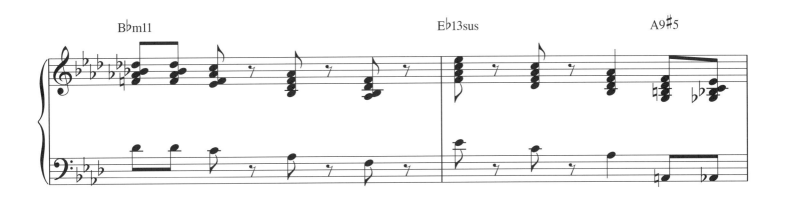

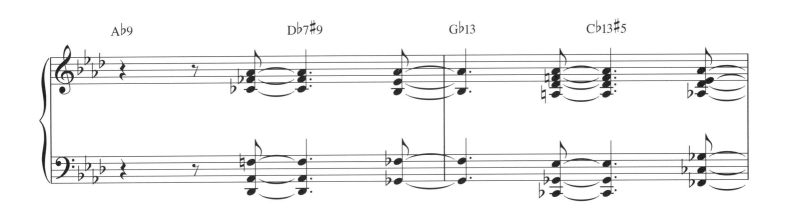

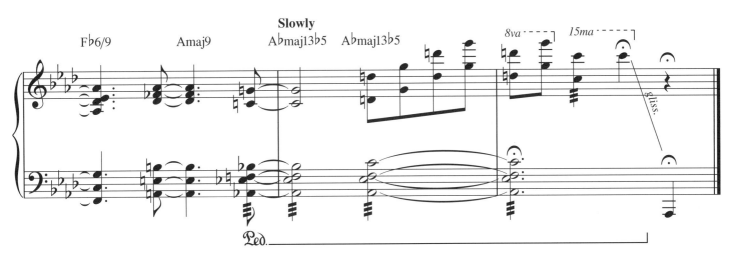

That Old Black Magic

from the Paramount Picture STAR SPANGLED RHYTHM

Words by Johnny Mercer
Music by Harold Arlen

Bright Swing ♩ = 200

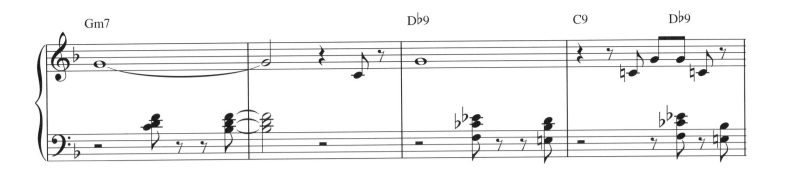

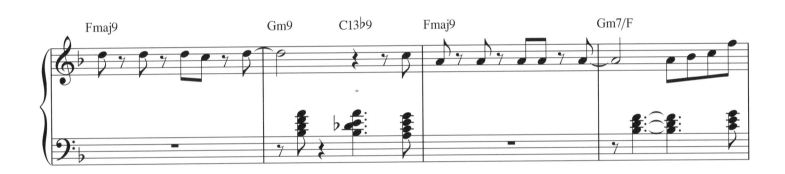

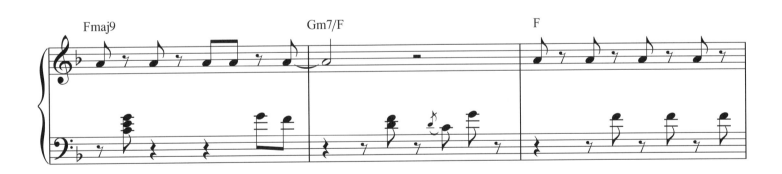

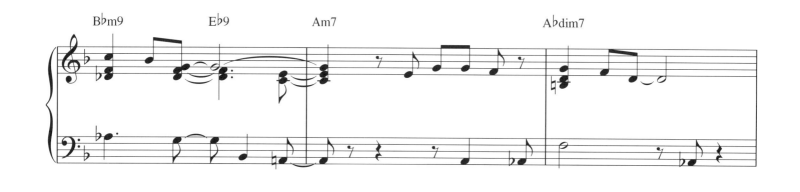

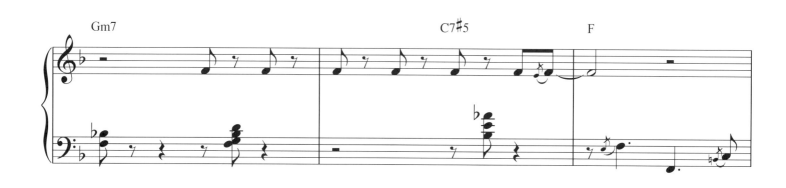

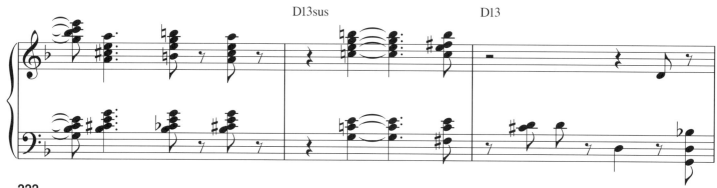

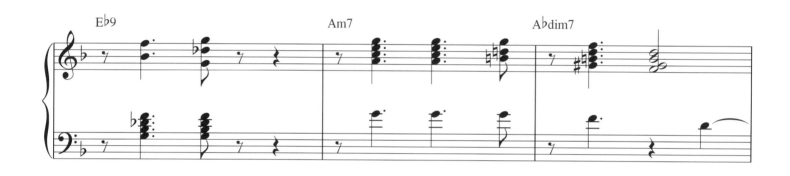

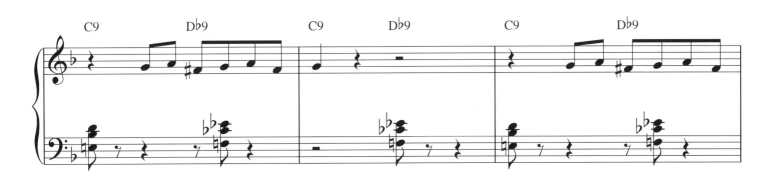

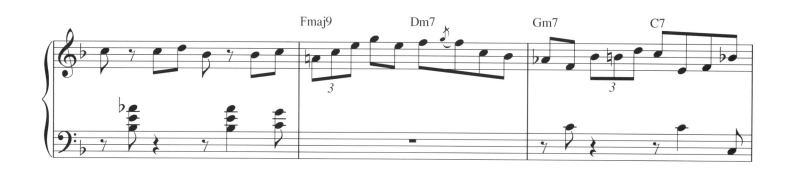

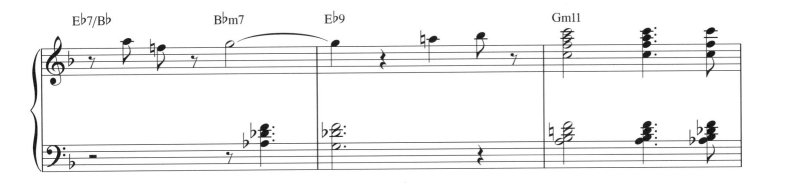

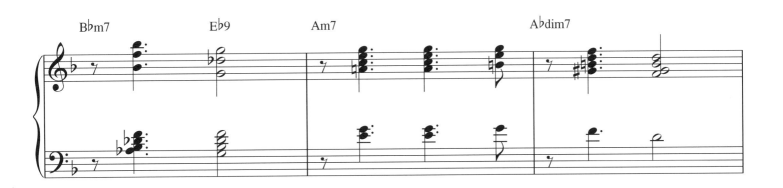

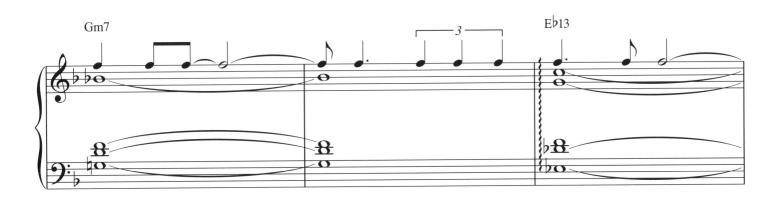

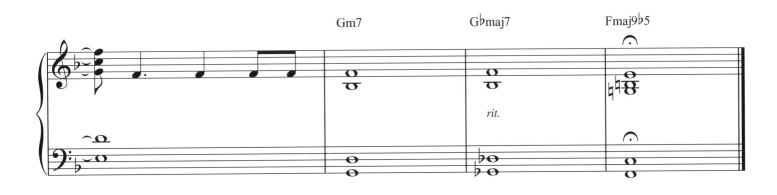

Watch What Happens

from THE UMBRELLAS OF CHERBOURG

Music by Michel Legrand
Original French Text by Jacques Demy
English Lyrics by Norman Gimbel

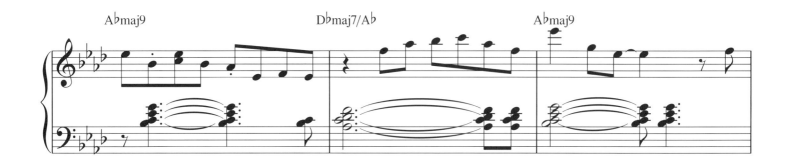

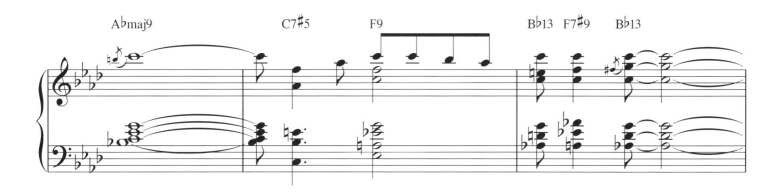

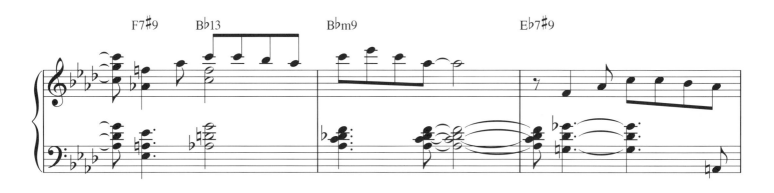

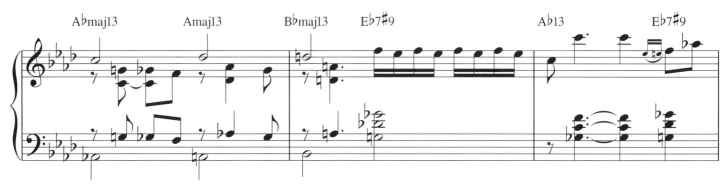

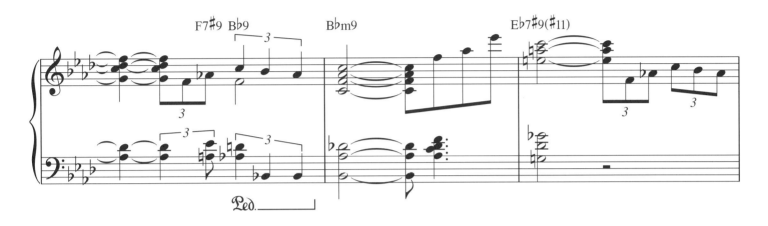

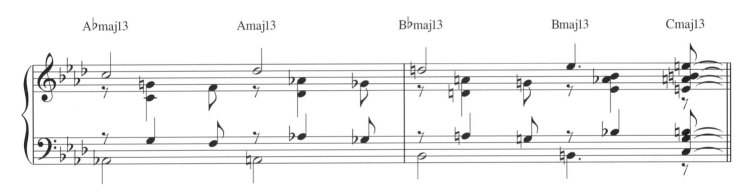

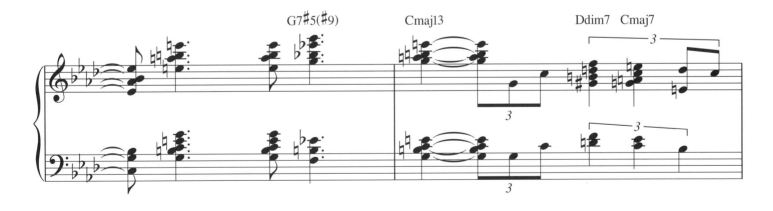

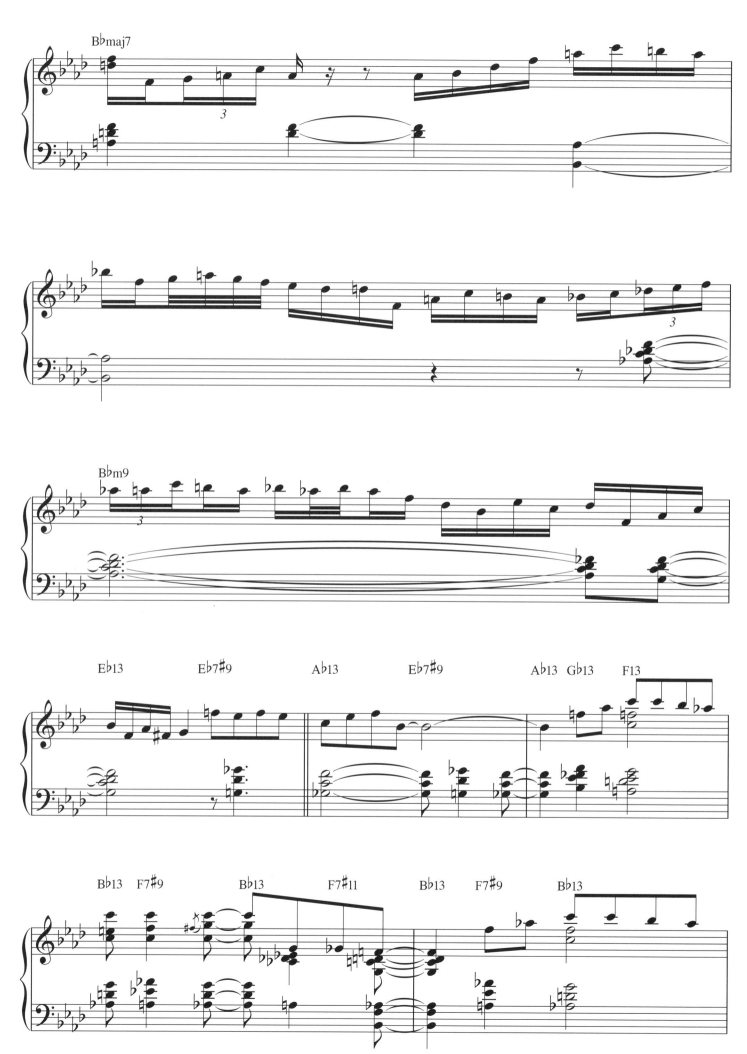

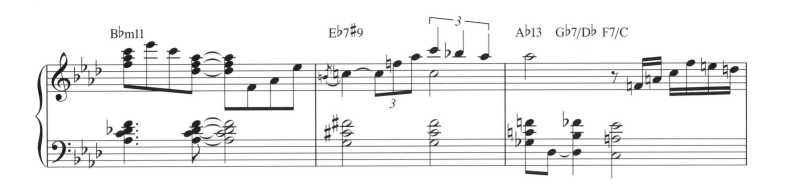

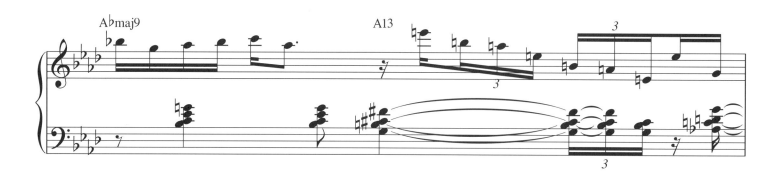

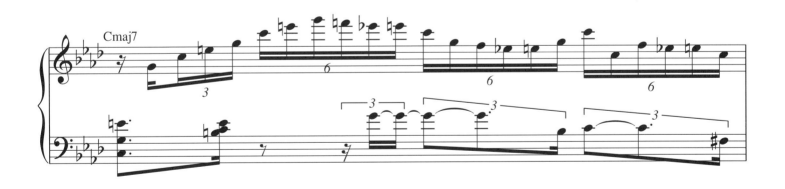

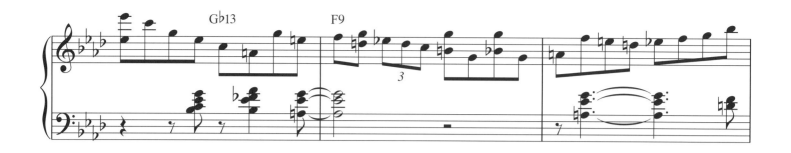

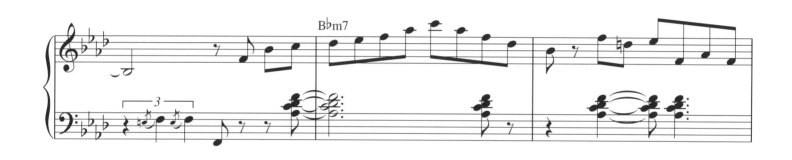

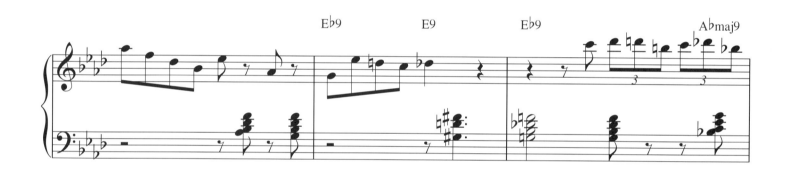

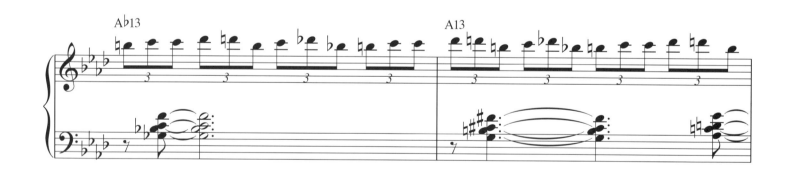

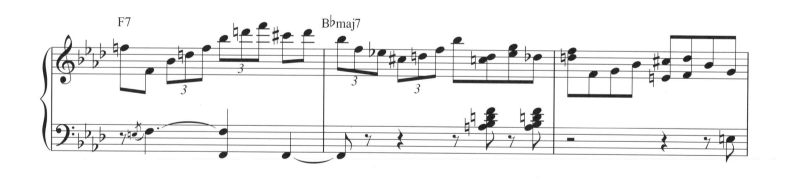

244

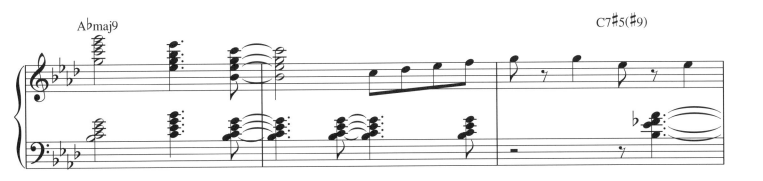

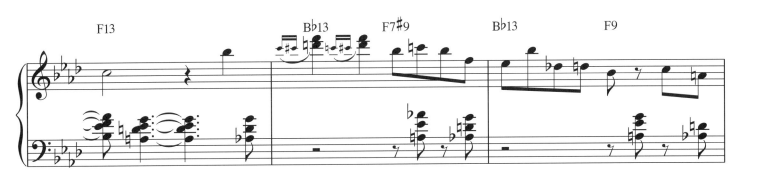

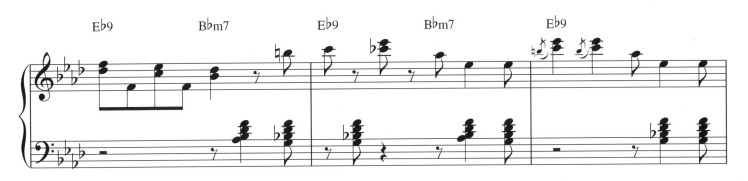

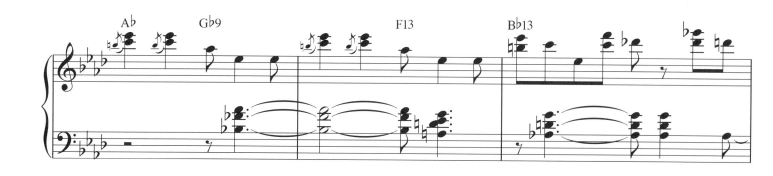

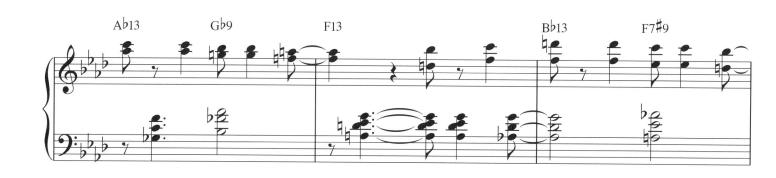

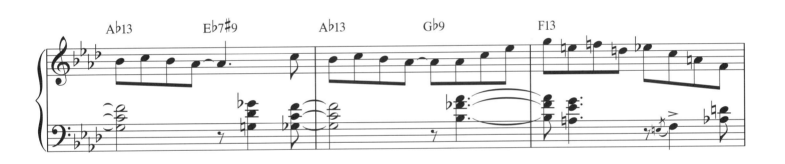

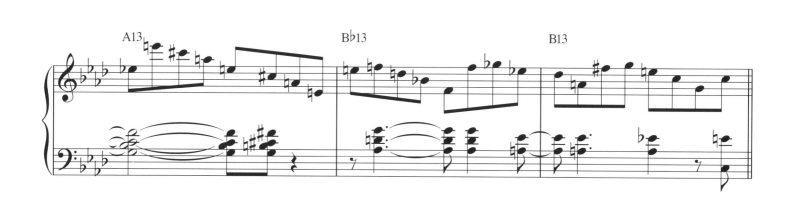

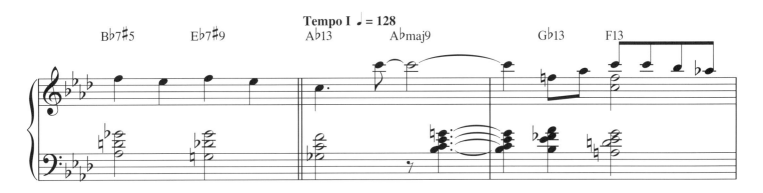

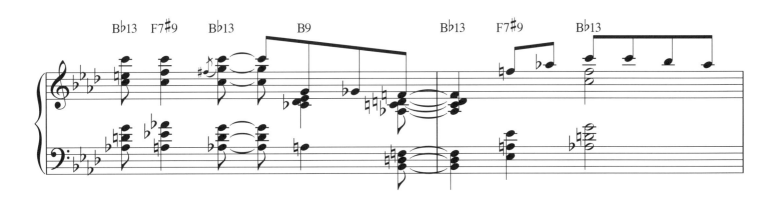

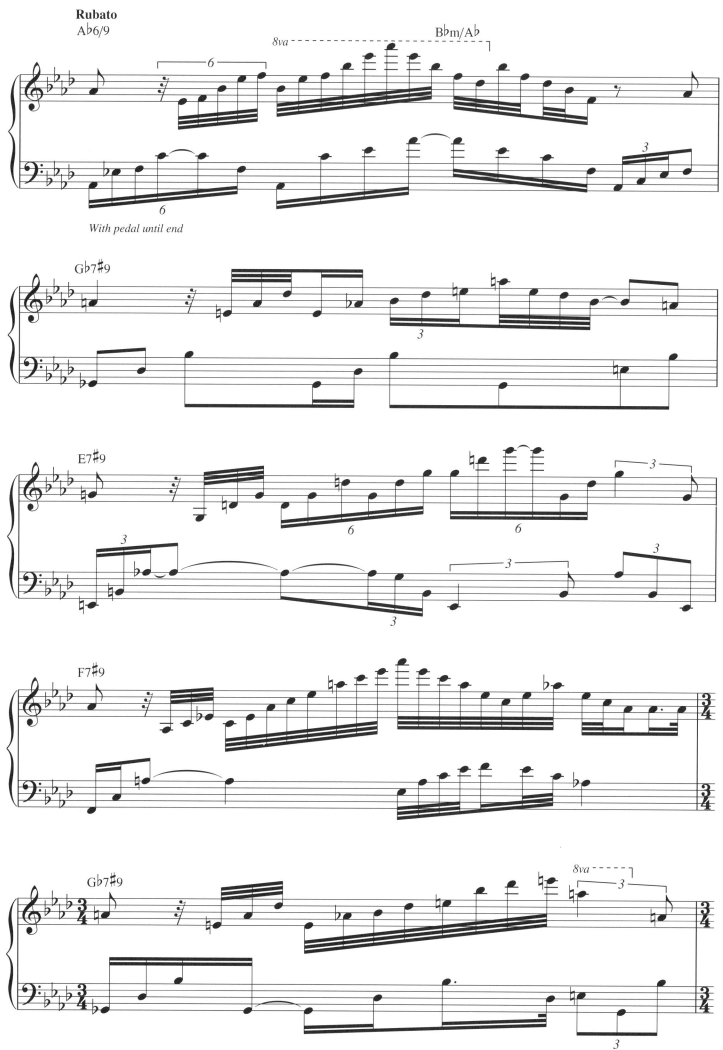

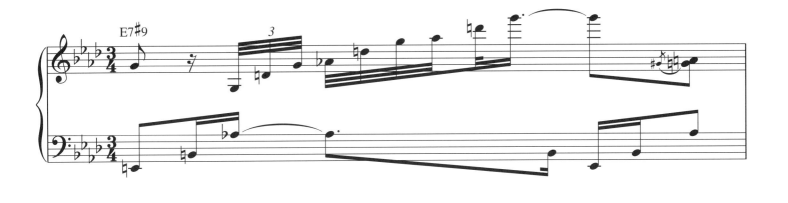

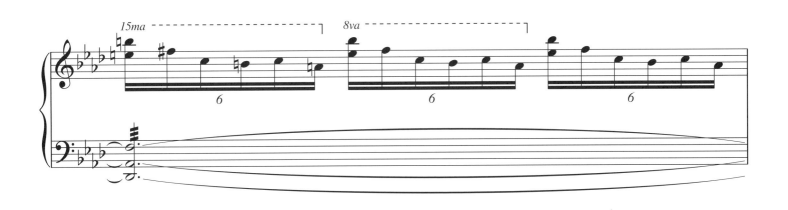

Witchcraft

Lyric by Carolyn Leigh
Music by Cy Coleman

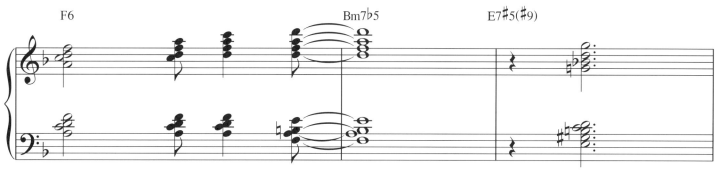

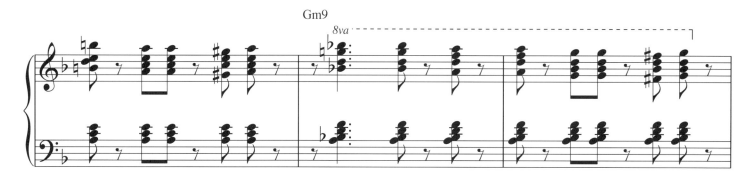

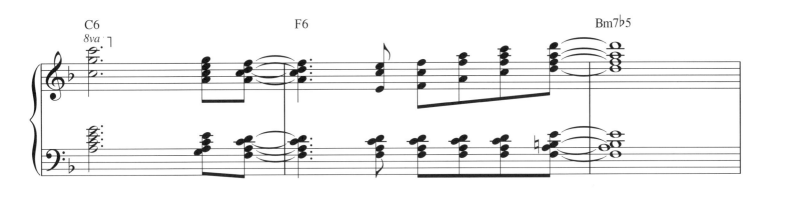

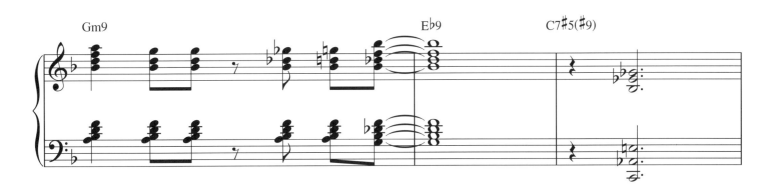

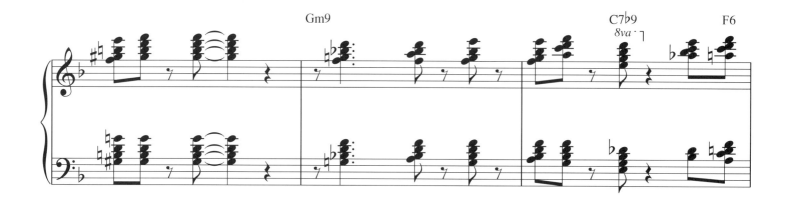

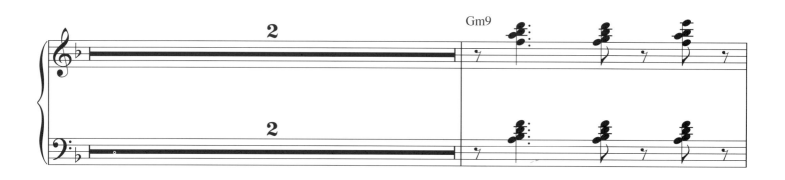

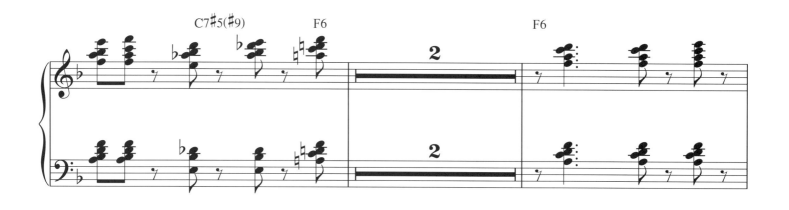

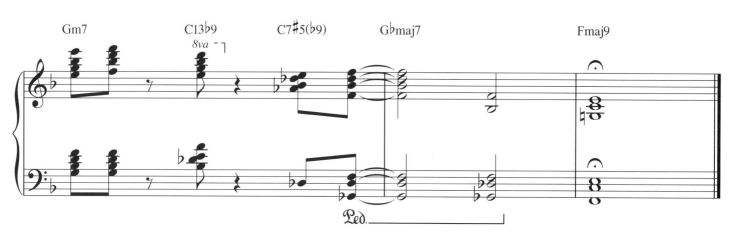

Yesterdays

from ROBERTA

Words by Otto Harbach
Music by Jerome Kern

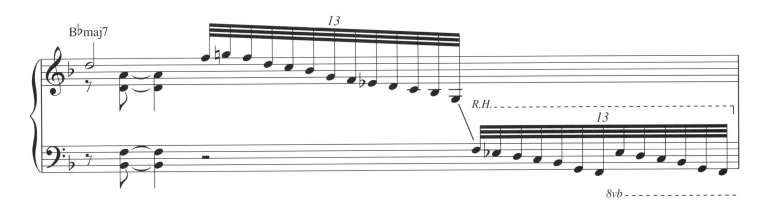

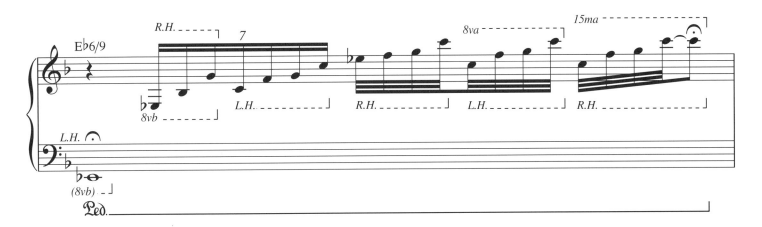

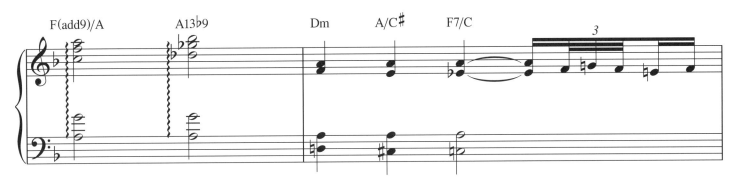

260

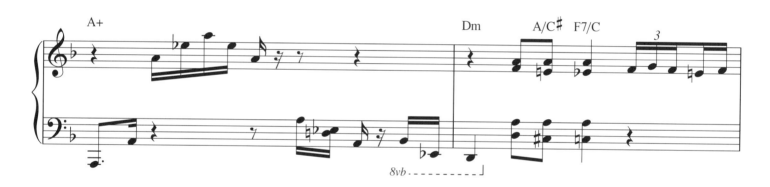

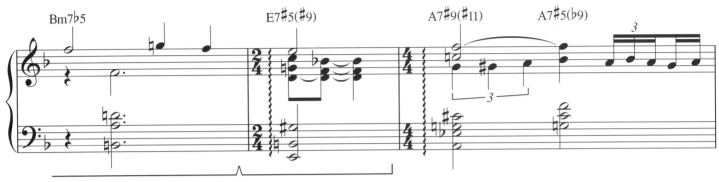

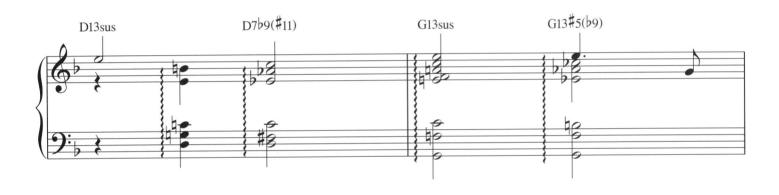

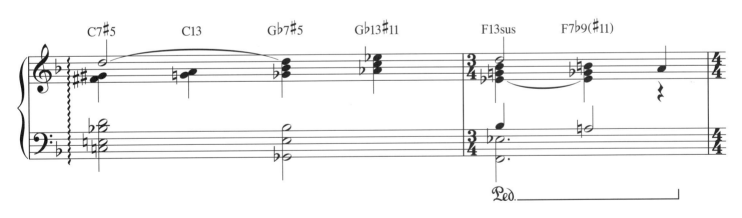

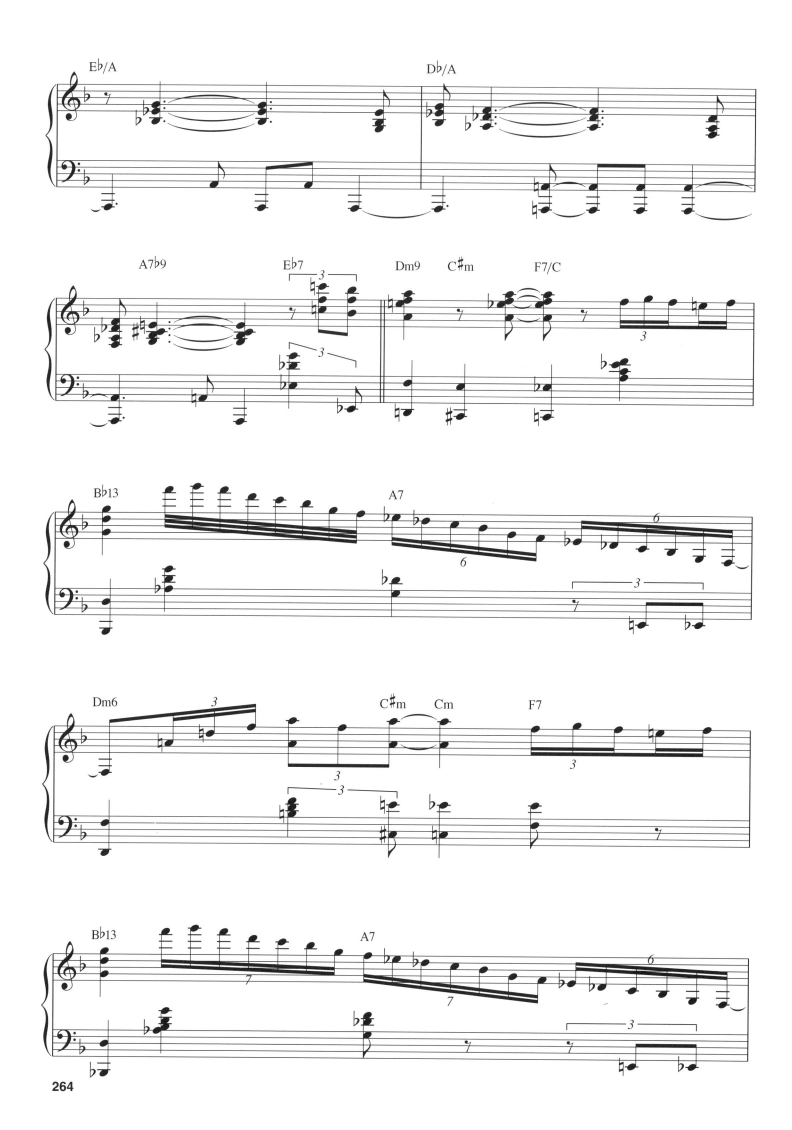

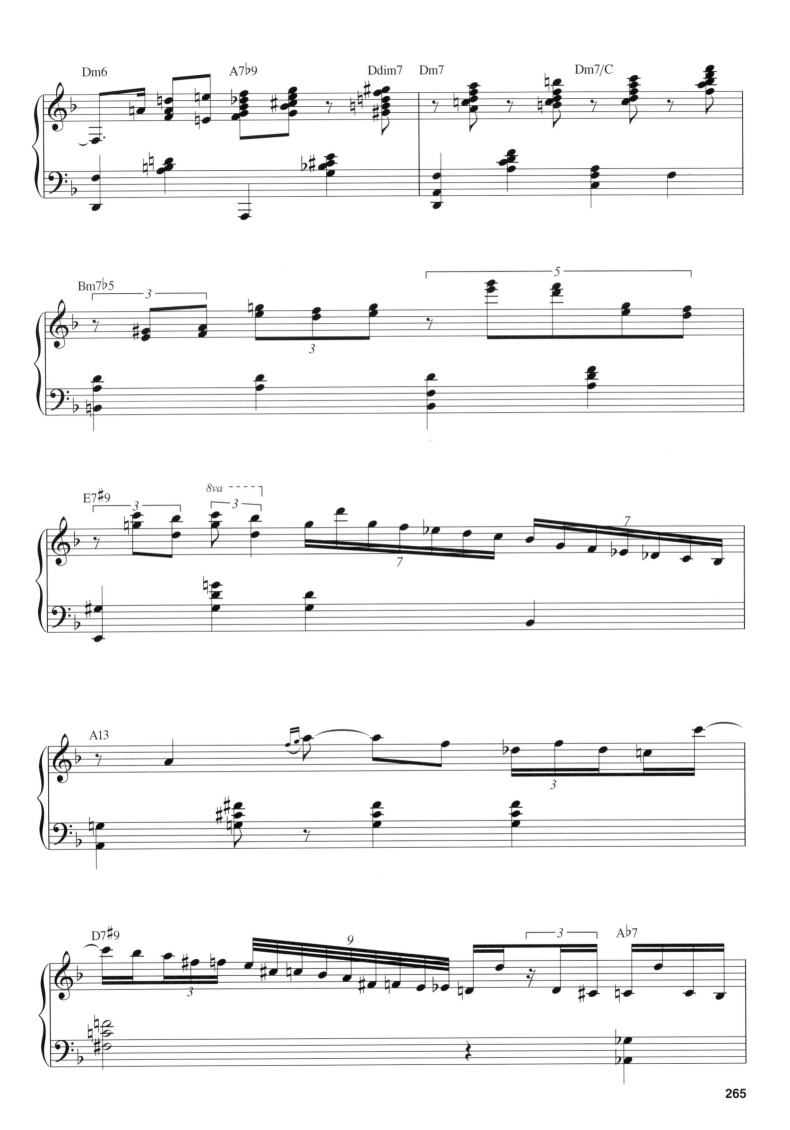

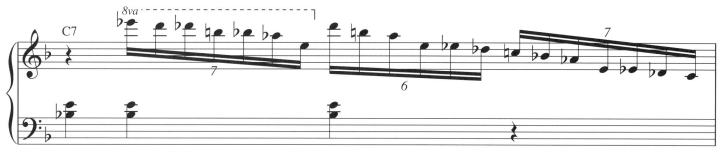

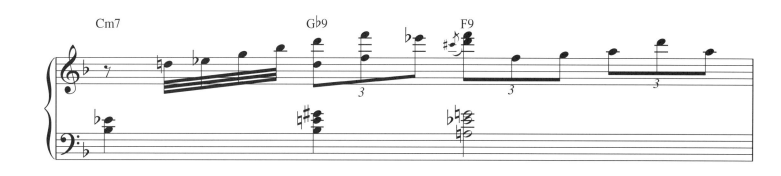

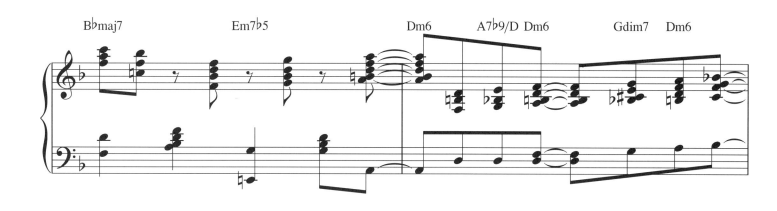

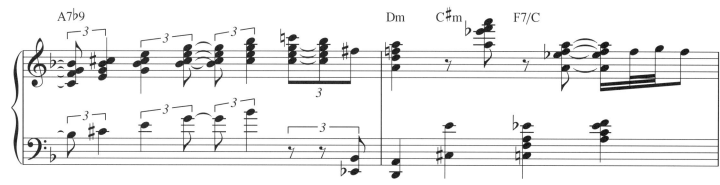

Oscar Peterson
Discography

Alice in Wonderland
Exclusively for My Friends
(Verve 314 513 830-2)

Blues Etude
Blues Etude
(Limelight 818 844-2)

Cheek to Cheek
The Song Is You: Best of the Verve Songbooks
(Verve 314 531 558-2)

Emily
The London Concert
(Pablo 2620-111-2)

Hymn to Freedom
The Oscar Peterson Trio in Tokyo, 1964
(Pablo MW 9055/6)

Indiana
The Oscar Peterson Trio at the Concertgebouw
(Verve 314 521 649-2)

It's Only a Paper Moon
Oscar Peterson Plays the
Harold Arlen Song Book
(Verve 314 589 103-2)

Jitterbug Waltz
The London Concert
(Pablo 2620-111-2)

Laura
The Oscar Peterson Trio at Zardi's
(Pablo 2620-118-2)

Lover
The Song Is You: Best of the Verve Songbooks
(Verve 314 531 558-2)

Misty
Eloquence: The Oscar Peterson Trio
Live at the Tivoli Gardens, Copenhagen
(Limelight 818 842-2)

Night and Day
Oscar Peterson Plays the
Cole Porter Song Book
(Verve 821 987-2)

Quiet Nights of Quiet Stars
We Get Requests
(Verve 314 521 442-2)

Tangerine
The Jazz Soul of Oscar Peterson/Affinity
(Verve 314 533 100-2)

Teach Me Tonight
Two Originals
(Verve 314 533 549-2)

That Old Black Magic
The Song Is You: Best of the Verve Songbooks
(Verve 314 531 558-2)

Watch What Happens
Tristeza on Piano
(Polygram 817489)

Witchcraft
A Jazz Portrait of Frank Sinatra
(Verve 422 825 769-2)

Yesterdays
The Song Is You: Best of the Verve Songbooks
(Verve 314 531 558-2)

MORE PUBLICATIONS FEATURING
OSCAR PETERSON

 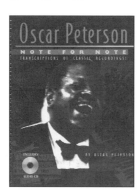   

OSCAR PETERSON

PG Music Inc.

In this breakthrough CD-ROM, Peterson takes you on an exciting musical journey through his life and career, integrating interactive audio/visual performances with on-screen piano display and notation. There is a full range of playback features to slow the tempo, step through each piece note by note, loop, or transpose to your favorite key. Includes 14 performances by Peterson (The Smudge • City Lights • Hogtown Blues • Place St-Henri • Blues for Scoti • and more), 10 MIDI transcriptions of his famous blues performances, live video and audio commentary, an interactive autobiography, a complete discography, a time line, a photo gallery, a helpful user's guide, and much more!

00451047 CD-ROM $79.95

OSCAR PETERSON – THE CLASSIC TRIOS

Keyboard Signature Licks

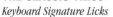

Learn how to play piano in the style of Oscar Peterson! Analyzes 14 of his trademark pieces: C-Jam Blues • Cheek to Cheek • Come Rain or Come Shine • Do Nothin' Till You Hear from Me • Don't Get Around Much Anymore • The Girl from Ipanema • I Got It Bad and That Ain't Good • The Lady Is a Tramp • My One and Only Love • Quiet Nights of Quiet Stars • Take the "A" Train • That Old Black Magic • and more.

00695871 Book/CD Pack $22.95

OSCAR PETERSON – JAZZ EXERCISES, MINUETS, ETUDES & PIECES FOR PIANO

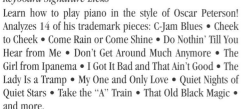

Legendary jazz pianist Oscar Peterson has long been devoted to the education of piano students. In this book he offers dozens of pieces designed to empower the student, whether novice or classically trained, with the technique needed to become an accomplished jazz pianist.

00311225 ....$9.95

OSCAR PETERSON – JAZZ PIANO SOLOS

Includes 8 Peterson classics for jazz piano: The Continental • Gravy Waltz • Hallelujah Time • Hymn to Freedom • Roundalay • Smedley's Blues • The Smudge • The Strut.

00672542 Piano Transcriptions $14.95

OSCAR PETERSON: THE LIFE OF A LEGEND

featuring Quincy Jones, Dizzy Gillespie, Ella Fitzgerald, Norman Granz and more

VIEW Video

In Peterson's own articulate voice we hear stories of the man who made the music and the times that made the man: making history with Norman Granz's *Jazz at the Philharmonic,* the clashes with racism that faced him and his racially-mixed trio, and a lifetime of performances with a who's-who of jazz. Insightful moments at the Peterson family's reunion disclose the personal price of greatness paid by Oscar and his relatives, distanced by the pianist's commitment to his music and his years of life on the road. A personal look at a technical virtuoso and master of swing whose life has been shaped by the ambition to honor his father's credo: "Be the best." 2 Tapes – 51 minutes each.

00320284 2-Video Set $29.95

OSCAR PETERSON – MUSIC IN THE KEY OF OSCAR

with Ella Fitzgerald, Dizzy Gillespie, Quincy Jones, Norman Granz and more

VIEW Video

Oscar Peterson: Music in the Key of Oscar is a music documentary that traces the history of this piano legend from his early days as Montreal's teenage boogie-woogie sensation through his rise to international celebrity. Highlights include: Caravan • Tenderly • Nigerian Marketplace • and more!

00320077 Two-Video Set $29.95

OSCAR PETERSON

PG Music Inc.

This fabulous book/CD pack features transcriptions of 18 piano solos by the legendary Oscar Peterson, taken directly from the original recordings. The solos are divided into two groups: eight (Chicago Blues • Hymn to Freedom • Nightingale • Night Time • and more) and ten selections in *Oscar Peterson Plays the Blues* (Blues Etude • Greasy Blues • Oscar's Boogie • R.B. Blues • Ron's Blues • and more). Includes an intro by the editor complete with performance notes, a welcome letter from Oscar Peterson and great photos, with Oscar's captions, throughout. The CD contains performances of each transcription played by gifted jazz pianist Miles Black.

00294030 Book/CD Pack $39.95

OSCAR PETERSON ORIGINALS

TRANSCRIPTIONS, LEAD SHEETS AND PERFORMANCE NOTES

5 original Peterson compositions transcribed for piano: The Cakewalk • The Gentle Waltz • He Has Gone • Love Ballade • Sushi.

00672544 Piano Transcriptions $9.95

OSCAR PETERSON PLAYS BROADWAY

18 songs arranged for piano: All the Things You Are • Baubles, Bangles and Beads • Body and Soul • Come Rain or Come Shine • Easter Parade • If I Were a Bell • Just in Time • The Lady Is a Tramp • Maria • On a Clear Day • People • Strike up the Band • Summertime • The Surrey with the Fringe on Top • There's a Small Hotel • 'Til Tomorrow • Who Can I Turn To • Wouldn't It Be Lovely.

00672532 Piano Transcriptions $19.95

OSCAR PETERSON PLAYS DUKE ELLINGTON

17 transcriptions of one of the greatest piano players of our time performing the works of one of the greatest composers of our time. Includes: Band Call • C-Jam Blues • Caravan • Cotton Tail • Do Nothin' Till You Hear from Me • Don't Get Around Much Anymore • I Got It Bad and That Ain't Good • In a Mellow Tone • John Hardy's Wife • Just a Settin' and a Rockin' • Night Train • Prelude to a Kiss • Rockin' in Rhythm • Satin Doll • Sophisticated Lady • Take the "A" Train • Things Ain't What They Used to Be.

00672531 Piano Transcriptions $19.95

OSCAR PETERSON TRIO – CANADIANA SUITE

In 1964 Oscar Peterson wrote a collection of compositions inspired by towns and regions in his native Canada. The resulting *Canadiana Suite* includes: Ballad to the East • Blues of the Prairies • Hogtown Blues • Land of the Misty Giants • Laurentide Waltz • March Past • Place St. Henri • Wheatland.

00672543 Piano Transcriptions $7.95

OSCAR PETERSON TRIOS

20 authentic transcriptions, including: Blues Etude • Hymn to Freedom • Misty • Quiet Nights of Quiet Stars • Witchcraft • and more.

00672533 Piano Transcriptions $24.95

THE VERY BEST OF OSCAR PETERSON

18 transcriptions from one of the greatest and most revered jazz pianists, including: A Child Is Born • The Continental • Gravy Waltz • I'm Old Fashioned • It Ain't Necessarily So • Little Girl Blue • Love Is Here to Stay • Moanin' • My One and Only Love • Noreen's Nocturne • On the Trail • Over the Rainbow • Place St. Henri • Rockin' Chair • 'Round Midnight • Stella by Starlight • Sweet Georgia Brown • That's All.

00672534 Piano Transcriptions $19.95

FOR MORE INFORMATION, SEE YOUR LOCAL MUSIC DEALER, OR WRITE TO:

7777 W. BLUEMOUND RD. P.O. BOX 13819 MILWAUKEE, WI 53213

Prices, contents and availability subject to change without notice.

Visit Hal Leonard Online at
www.halleonard.com

0505

ARTIST TRANSCRIPTIONS®

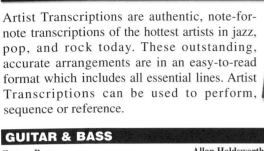

Artist Transcriptions are authentic, note-for-note transcriptions of the hottest artists in jazz, pop, and rock today. These outstanding, accurate arrangements are in an easy-to-read format which includes all essential lines. Artist Transcriptions can be used to perform, sequence or reference.

GUITAR & BASS

George Benson
00660113 Guitar Style of $14.95

Pierre Bensusan
00699072 Guitar Book of.................$19.95

Ron Carter
00672331 Acoustic Bass.................$16.95

Stanley Clarke
00672307 The Collection.................$19.95

Al Di Meola
00604041 Cielo E Terra $14.95
00660115 Friday Night in
                San Francisco...............$14.95
00604043 Music, Words, Pictures....$14.95

Tal Farlow
00673245 Jazz Style of $19.95

Bela Fleck and the Flecktones
00672359 Melody/Lyrics/Chords.....$18.95

Frank Gambale
00672336 Best of $22.95

Jim Hall
00699389 Jazz Guitar Environments ..$19.95
00699306 Exploring Jazz Guitar $17.95

Allan Holdsworth
00604049 Reaching for the
                Uncommon Chord $14.95

Leo Kottke
00699215 Eight Songs $14.95

Wes Montgomery
00675536 Guitar Transcriptions $17.95

Joe Pass
00672353 The Collection.................$18.95

John Patitucci
00673216 ....$14.95

Django Reinhardt
00027083 Anthology $14.95
00026711 The Genius of $10.95
00026715 A Treasury of Songs $12.95

Johnny Smith
00672374 Guitar Solos $16.95

Mike Stern
00673224 Guitar Book.....................$16.95

Mark Whitfield
00672320 Guitar Collection.............$19.95

Gary Willis
00672337 The Collection.................$19.95

SAXOPHONE

Julian "Cannonball" Adderley
00673244 The Collection.................$19.95

Michael Brecker
00673237 ....$19.95
00672429 The Collection.................$19.95

The Brecker Brothers
00672351 And All Their Jazz............$19.95
00672447 Best of $19.95

Benny Carter
00672314 The Collection.................$22.95
00672315 Plays Standards $22.95

James Carter
00672394 The Collection.................$19.95

John Coltrane
00672494 A Love Supreme $12.95
00672529 Giant Steps.....................$14.95
00672493 Plays Coltrane Changes..$19.95
00672349 Plays Giant Steps $19.95
00672453 Plays Standards $19.95
00673233 Solos...............................$22.95

Paul Desmond
00672328 The Collection.................$19.95
00672454 Standard Time $19.95

Kenny Garrett
00672530 The Collection.................$19.95

Stan Getz
00699375 ....$18.95
00672377 Bossa Novas $19.95
00672375 Standards $17.95

Coleman Hawkins
00672523 The Collection.................$19.95

Joe Henderson
00672330 Best of $22.95
00673252 Selections from Lush Life
                & So Near So Far $19.95

Kenny G
00673239 Best of $19.95
00673229 Breathless.......................$19.95
00672462 Classics in the Key of G ..$19.95
00672485 Faith: A Holiday Album....$14.95
00672373 The Moment $19.95
00672516 Paradise $14.95

Joe Lovano
00672326 The Collection.................$19.95

Jackie McLean
00672498 The Collection.................$19.95

James Moody
00672372 The Collection $19.95

Frank Morgan
00672416 The Collection.................$19.95

Sonny Rollins
00672444 The Collection.................$19.95

David Sanborn
00675000 The Collection.................$16.95

Bud Shank
00672528 The Collection.................$19.95

Wayne Shorter
00672498 New Best of $19.95

Lew Tabackin
00672455 The Collection.................$19.95

Stanley Turrentine
00672334 The Collection.................$19.95

Lester Young
00672524 The Collection.................$19.95

PIANO & KEYBOARD

Monty Alexander
00672338 The Collection.................$19.95
00672487 Plays Standards $19.95

Kenny Barron
00672318 The Collection.................$22.95

Count Basie
00672520 The Collection.................$19.95

Warren Bernhardt
00672364 The Collection.................$19.95

Cyrus Chesnut
00672439 The Collection.................$19.95

Billy Childs
00673242 The Collection.................$19.95

Chick Corea
00672300 Paint the World $12.95

Bill Evans
00672537 At Town Hall $16.95
00672365 The Collection.................$19.95
00672425 Piano Interpretations........$19.95
00672510 Trio, Vol. 1: 1959-1961 ....$24.95
00672511 Trio, Vol. 2: 1962-1965 ....$24.95
00672512 Trio, Vol. 3: 1968-1974 ....$24.95
00672513 Trio, Vol. 4: 1979-1980 ....$24.95

Benny Goodman
00672492 The Collection.................$16.95

Benny Green
00672329 The Collection.................$19.95

Vince Guaraldi
00672486 The Collection.................$19.95

Herbie Hancock
00672419 The Collection.................$19.95

Gene Harris
00672446 The Collection.................$19.95

Hampton Hawes
00672438 The Collection.................$19.95

Ahmad Jamal
00672322 The Collection.................$22.95

CLARINET

Buddy De Franco
00672423 The Collection.................$19.95

FLUTE

Eric Dolphy
00672379 The Collection.................$19.95

James Moody
00672372 The Collection $19.95

James Newton
00660108 Improvising Flute $14.95

Lew Tabackin
00672455 The Collection.................$19.95

TROMBONE

J.J. Johnson
00672332 The Collection.................$19.95

PIANO & KEYBOARD (continued)

Brad Mehldau
00672476 The Collection.................$19.95

Thelonious Monk
00672388 Best of $19.95
00672389 The Collection.................$19.95
00672390 Jazz Standards, Vol. 1 ....$19.95
00672391 Jazz Standards, Vol. 2 ....$19.95
00672392 Intermediate Piano Solos..$14.95

Jelly Roll Morton
00672433 The Piano Rolls...............$12.95

Oscar Peterson
00672531 Plays Duke Ellington........$19.95
00672534 Very Best of $19.95

Michael Petrucciani
00673226 ....$17.95

Bud Powell
00672371 Classics $19.95
00672376 The Collection.................$19.95

André Previn
00672437 The Collection.................$19.95

Gonzalo Rubalcaba
00672507 The Collection.................$19.95

Horace Silver
00672303 The Collection.................$19.95

Art Tatum
00672316 The Collection.................$22.95
00672355 Solo Book $19.95

Billy Taylor
00672357 The Collection.................$24.95

McCoy Tyner
00673215 ....$16.95

Cedar Walton
00672321 The Collection.................$19.95

Kenny Werner
00672519 The Collection.................$19.95

Teddy Wilson
00672434 The Collection.................$19.95

TRUMPET

Louis Armstrong
00672480 The Collection.................$14.95
00672481 Plays Standards $14.95

Chet Baker
00672435 The Collection.................$19.95

Randy Brecker
00673234 ....$17.95

The Brecker Brothers
00672351 And All Their Jazz............$19.95
00672447 Best of $19.95

Miles Davis
00672448 Originals, Vol. 1 ....$19.95
00672451 Originals, Vol. 2 ....$19.95
00672450 Standards, Vol. 1 ....$19.95
00672449 Standards, Vol. 2 ....$19.95

Dizzy Gillespie
00672479 The Collection.................$19.95

Freddie Hubbard
00673214 ....$14.95

Tom Harrell
00672382 Jazz Trumpet Solos $19.95

Chuck Mangione
00672506 The Collection.................$19.95